Mike McGrath

PHP

in
easy steps

Fourth Edition

In easy steps is an imprint of In Easy Steps Limited
16 Hamilton Terrace · Holly Walk · Leamington Spa
Warwickshire · United Kingdom · CV32 4LY
www.ineasysteps.com

Fourth Edition

In Easy Steps Limited supports The Forest Stewardship Council (FSC),
the leading international forest certification organization. All our titles
that are printed on Greenpeace approved FSC certified paper carry the
FSC logo.

MIX
Paper from
responsible sources
FSC® C020837

Printed and bound in the United Kingdom

ISBN 978-1-84078-923-2

Contents

1 Getting started   7

Introducing PHP	8
Installing the Abyss server	10
Installing the PHP engine	12
Integrating Abyss and PHP	14
Embedding PHP script code	16
Scripting by the rules	18
Improving performance	20
Enabling JIT compilation	22
Summary	24

2 Storing values   25

Creating variables	26
Quoting strings	28
Producing arrays	30
Sorting arrays	32
Describing dimensions	34
Checking types	36
Defining constants	38
Exploring superglobals	40
Summary	42

3 Performing operations   43

Doing arithmetic	44
Making comparisons	46
Examining conditions	48
Assessing logic	50
Comparing bits	52
Changing values	54
Grasping precedence	55
Summary	56

4 Testing conditions   57

Seeking truth	58
Providing alternatives	60
Switching branches	62
Matching expressions	64
Performing loops	66

Looping while true 68
Breaking from loops 70
Summary 72

5 Employing functions 73

Defining functions 74
Passing arguments 76
Varying parameters 78
Naming parameters 80
Recognizing scope 82
Returning values 84
Allowing union types 86
Calling back 88
Summary 90

6 Manipulating strings 91

Comparing characters 92
Searching text 94
Extracting substrings 96
Changing case 97
Formatting strings 98
Making dates 100
Encoding entities 102
Summary 104

7 Building classes 105

Encapsulating data 106
Creating an object 108
Initializing members 110
Using constructors 112
Promoting properties 114
Inheriting properties 116
Embracing polymorphism 118
Chaining method calls 120
Summary 122

8 Handling files 123

Reading files 124
Reading lines 126
Reading characters 127
Writing a file 128
Appending text 130

Handling errors   132
Catching exceptions   134
Summary   136

9   Producing forms   137

Performing actions   138
Checking set values   140
Validating form data   142
Filtering data   144
Sending hidden data   146
Handling submissions   148
Making sticky forms   150
Uploading files   152
Surrounding forms   154
Appending link data   156
Summary   158

10   Preserving data   159

Submitting cookie data   160
Setting cookies   161
Getting cookies   162
Viewing cookie data   164
Submitting session data   166
Setting sessions   167
Getting sessions   168
Viewing session data   170
Summary   172

11   Adding Web Services   173

Loading data   174
Getting nodes   176
Getting attributes   178
Including feeds   180
Setting parameters   182
Selecting components   184
Summary   186

Index   187

How to Use This Book

The examples in this book demonstrate features of the PHP scripting language, and the screenshots illustrate the actual results produced by the listed code examples. Certain colorization conventions are used to clarify the code listed in the steps...

Components of the PHP language are colored blue, programmer-specified names are colored red, literal text and numeric values are black, and code comments are green, like this:

```php
<?php

    # Write the traditional greeting.
    $greeting = 'Hello World!' ;
    echo "<h1>$greeting</h1>" ;

?>
```

Additionally, in order to identify each source code file described in the steps, a file icon and file name appears in the margin alongside the steps:

| script.php | page.html | style.css | data.xml | text.txt | image.png |

Grab the Source Code

For convenience, the source code files from all examples featured in this book are available in a single ZIP archive. You can obtain this archive by following these easy steps:

1. Browse to **www.ineasysteps.com** then navigate to Free Resources and choose the Downloads section

2. Next, find PHP in easy steps, 4th edition in the list, then click on the hyperlink entitled All Code Examples to download the ZIP archive file

3. Now, extract the archive contents to the web server's **/htdocs** directory on your PC

If you don't achieve the result illustrated in any example, simply compare your code to that in the original example files you have downloaded to discover where you went wrong.

1 Getting started

Welcome to the exciting

world of the interactive

web with PHP. This chapter

demonstrates how to create

a dynamic development

environment with a web

server and the PHP engine.

8   Introducing PHP

10 Installing the Abyss server

12 Installing the PHP engine

14 Integrating Abyss and PHP

16 Embedding PHP script code

18 Scripting by the rules

20 Improving performance

22 Enabling JIT compilation

24 Summary

This is the official logo of the PHP project – the official online home of PHP can be found at **php.net**

Introducing PHP

The most appealing modern websites provide a customized user experience by dynamically responding to some current conditions – user name, time of day, latest blog, shopping cart contents, etc. Many of these dynamic websites are created using PHP.

What is PHP?

PHP is a widely-used general purpose scripting language that is especially suited for web development and can be embedded into HTML. It was created by programmer Rasmus Lerdorf, as a set of scripts to maintain his website that he released as "Personal Home Page Tools (PHP Tools) version 1.0" on June 8, 1995.

The tools were extended in the version 2 release of 1997, and the name changed to become a recursive acronym "PHP: Hypertext Preprocessor" in version 3 the following year. Performance, reliability and extensibility were improved in 2000 with the release of PHP4, which was powered by the Zend engine virtual machine.

Subsequently, PHP5 was released in 2004 powered by the new Zend II engine and produced as free software by the PHP group. A planned experimental version PHP6, which intended to introduce native Unicode support throughout PHP, was abandoned but PHP7 was released in 2015. PHP8 was released in 2020 and offers "Just In Time" (JIT) compilation for improved performance. Today, PHP is installed on over 20 million websites and 1 million web servers.

Why is PHP popular?

This is the "elePHPant" – the mascot of the PHP project, designed by Vincent Pontier.

- PHP is extremely simple for a newcomer, but offers many advanced features for a professional programmer.

- PHP code is enclosed in special start and end processing tags that allow you to jump into and out of "PHP mode", to implement instructions within an HTML document.

- PHP code is executed on the server ("server-side"), unlike JavaScript code that is executed in the browser ("client-side"). The client receives the results of running the script without knowing what the underlying code was. Recently, server-side has become known as "The Cloud".

Understanding The Cloud

Whenever a user asks to view a web page in their browser, it requests the page from the web server and receives the page in response, via the HTTP protocol. Where a web page contains PHP script, the web server will first call upon the PHP engine to process the code before sending the response to the web browser:

HTTP (HyperText Transfer Protocol) is the common communication standard that allows any computer connected to any web server to access files across the web.

The ensuing pages describe how to create a development environment for interactive websites by installing the following server-side technologies on your own computer:

- **Web Server** – Abyss Web Server X1

- **PHP Engine** – PHP 8 (8.0.1)

The examples in this book are created and tested with these software versions but may require modification for other versions.

Installing the Abyss server

Abyss X1 is a free compact web server available for Windows, macOS, and Linux operating systems available for download at **aprelium.com**
Despite its small footprint, Abyss supports many powerful features including dynamic content generation with server-side scripts – so is an ideal companion for PHP.

The Abyss Web Server can be installed on your own computer to provide an environment for interactive PHP website development:

Further guidance on installation of the Abyss Web Server is available at aprelium.com/abyssws/start.html

1 Download the Abyss X1 Web Server setup package for your system from **aprelium.com/abyssws/download.php**

2 Run the setup installer and **Agree** the License terms, then select the Abyss Web Server component and click **Next**

The Abyss setup package for Windows is an executable file named **abwsx1.exe** that you run to install the web server.

3 Accept the suggested location of **C:\Abyss Web Server** then choose to **Install as a Windows Service**

Abyss Web Server Startup Configuration

Select the startup method of Abyss Web Server:

○ Manual startup
○ Automatic startup on user logon
● Install as a Windows Service
  ☑ Start automatically on computer startup

OK   Cancel

After the installation process completes, your system's default web browser will open, displaying the Abyss Web Server Console.

Beware

If you choose the "Manual startup" option, the Abyss logo will not appear in your system tray for easy start/stop control and access to the server console. Instead, the console can be found with your browser at **http://localhost:9999** or numerically at **http://127.0.0.1:9999** ("localhost" is an alias for the IP address 127.0.0.1).

4 Select your preferred language, then enter a name and password for future access to the Abyss Console

5 Now, log in using your chosen name and password to see the Abyss Console confirm the server Status as "Running"

Abyss Web Server Console

Abyss Web Server Console

Abyss Web Server Console

Abyss Web Server Console   Help

Server Configuration   Console Configuration   Server Statistics   Server Activity   Help and Support   About Abyss Web Server

Host	Status		
Default Host On Port 80	Running	Stop	Configure
			Add

Hosts ⑦ :

Abyss Web Server X1

Hot tip

In the Abyss console, click the "Configure" button then the General icon to see the default HTTP Port is 80 and the default Documents Path (where your web pages will reside) is **/htdocs**.

6 Type **http://localhost** into your browser address field, then hit **Enter** – to see the default Abyss "Welcome" page

Welcome to Abyss Web Server

localhost

Welcome to Abyss Web Server

Abyss Web Server is running correctly on your system. You should now change this page with yours.

Please include in your web pages (at least the first) the *'Powered by Abyss Web Server'* banner to promote the use of the software.

Powered by Abyss Web Server

Installing the PHP engine

The PHP interpreter "engine", which implements PHP scripts within web pages, is available for Windows, macOS and Linux operating systems as a free download at **php.net**

 Open a web browser and navigate to **php.net**

 Next, choose the **Downloads** item on the page menu – to open a "Downloads" page

Further guidance on installation of PHP is available at **php.net/manual/en/install.php**

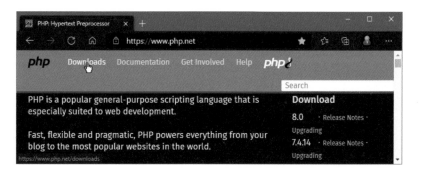

Now, select a package to download or select the **Windows downloads** link – to open a "Windows binaries" page

...cont'd

4 Then, click the **Zip** link to download a Thread Safe archive of PHP for 64-bit systems

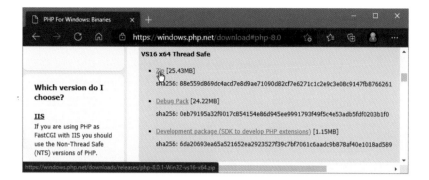

5 When the download completes, extract its contents to a convenient location on your system – such as **C:\PHP**

Hot tip

The PHP installation location will be required when configuring the Abyss Web Server to integrate with PHP – make a note of the Destination Folder.

Don't forget

Following installation of PHP, the web server cannot yet execute PHP scripts until it is configured to recognize them and to find the PHP interpreter engine – all as described on pages 14-15.

13

Further guidance on configuration of the Abyss Web Server is available online at aprelium.com/abyssws/ start.html

14

To clarify the code examples in this book, components of the PHP language are colored **blue**, programmer-specified names are **red**, numeric and string data is **black**, and comments are **green**.

The **localhost** domain name is an alias for the domain IP address of **127.0.0.1** – so the Abyss Web Server Console can alternatively be addressed as **http://127.0.0.1:9999**.

Integrating Abyss and PHP

The Abyss Web Server must be configured to recognize PHP scripts and employ the PHP interpreter when it encounters them. This is achieved in the Abyss Console by associating the file extension ".php" as being PHP scripts, and by specifying the location of the PHP engine on your system to interpret them:

1 Enter **http://localhost:9999** into your browser address field to launch the Abyss Web Server Console, then click the **Configure** button – to open the Configuration page

2 Click on the 🗔 **Scripting Parameters** icon – to open the Scripting Parameters page for editing

3 Ensure that the **Enable Scripts Execution** box is checked, then click the **Add** button in the Interpreters table – to open the Interpreters-Add page

4 Set the **Interface** parameter to "FastCGI (Local - Pipes)"

5 Set the **Interpreter** parameter to the PHP path location on your system of the **php-cgi.exe** file

6 Set the **Associated Extensions** parameter to "php", so your configuration should look like that shown below:

Interpreters - Edit - C:\PHP\php-cgi.exe

localhost:9999/hosts/host@0/edit/scripting/int...

Interpreters - Edit - C:\PHP\php-cgi.exe

Interface ⑦ :	FastCGI (Local - Pipes) ⌄
Interpreter ⑦ :	C:\PHP\php-cgi.exe Browse...
Arguments ⑦ :	
Advanced Parameters ⑦ :	Edit...

☑ Check for file existence before execution ⑦

Type ⑦ : Standard ⌄

☑ Use the associated extensions to automatically update the Script Paths ⑦

Extension		
Associated Extensions ⑦ :	php	✎ 🗑
Add

OK

...cont'd

7 Click the **OK** button to validate your new configuration

8 Click the **Restart** button that next appears, to apply the changes you have made to the Abyss configuration

Beware

Documents can only be interpreted by the PHP engine if served up by the web server using the HTTP protocol. You cannot simply open a PHP file in your browser directly. Always use the location **http://localhost/** to serve the examples in this book.

The Abyss Web Server should now be running on your system, correctly configured to recognize that documents having the **.php** file extension should be interpreted by the PHP engine. Configuration can now be tested by creating a simple PHP script for service to your web browser by Abyss:

1 Open a plain text editor and exactly type the script below
`<?php  phpinfo() ;  ?>`

2 Save the script as **phpinfo.php** in the Abyss document path directory, typically at **C:\Abyss Web Server\htdocs**

3 Exactly enter the location **http://localhost/phpinfo.php** into your web browser's address field to see Abyss serve up a web page containing your PHP version information

phpinfo.php

PHP Version 8.0.1	
System	Windows NT CODER-PC 10.0 build 19042 (Windows 10) AMD64
Build Date	Jan 5 2021 23:36:34
Build System	Microsoft Windows Server 2016 Standard [10.0.14393]
Compiler	Visual C++ 2019
Architecture	x64
Configure Command	cscript /nologo /e:jscript configure.js "--enable-snapshot-build" ...
Server API	CGI/FastCGI

Beware

PHP scripts are case-sensitive so you must copy the listed script using lowercase characters only.

15

Embedding PHP script code

hello.php

PHP script may be embedded within HTML documents – meaning PHP and HTML code can both happily co-exist in the same file. All embedded PHP code must be contained within **<?php** and **?>** tags so it can be readily recognized by the PHP engine for interpretation. Typically, the PHP code will write content into the body section of the HTML document, which is then sent to the web browser:

1 Launch a plain text editor and create this valid barebones HTML document with an empty body section

```
<!DOCTYPE HTML>
<html lang="en">
<head>
<meta charset="UTF-8">
<title>Getting Started In PHP</title>
</head>
<body>

</body>
</html>
```

2 Insert tags into the body section to contain PHP code

```
<?php

?>
```

3 Next, insert between the PHP tags a descriptive comment and a line of code to write content into the body section

```
# Write the traditional greeting.
echo '<h1>Hello World!</h1>' ;
```

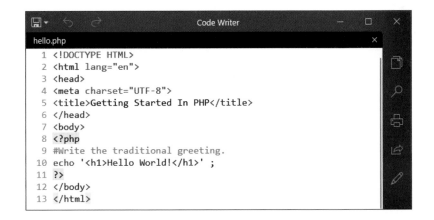

```
                                    Code Writer              —  □  ×
hello.php                                                           ×
 1  <!DOCTYPE HTML>
 2  <html lang="en">
 3  <head>
 4  <meta charset="UTF-8">
 5  <title>Getting Started In PHP</title>
 6  </head>
 7  <body>
 8  <?php
 9  #Write the traditional greeting.
10  echo '<h1>Hello World!</h1>' ;
11  ?>
12  </body>
13  </html>
```

Hot tip

Notice that the descriptive comment is enclosed between the PHP tags for information purposes only.

4   Save the document as **hello.php** in the Abyss web server's
/htdocs folder

5   Now, enter the location **http://localhost/hello.php** into your
web browser's address field – to see Abyss serve up a web
page containing content written by embedded PHP code

Getting Started In PHP   ×   +

← → C ⌂ ⓘ localhost/hello.php   ⊕ ☆ ❽ ⋮

Hello World!

6   Use your web browser's tools to inspect the page's source
code – to see that PHP has written the content into the
body section, including the HTML **<h1> </h1>** tags

Getting Started In PHP   ×   +

← → C ⌂ ⓘ localhost/hello.php   ⊕ ☆ ❽ ⋮

Hello World!

Back	Alt+Left Arrow
Forward	Alt+Right Arrow
Reload	Ctrl+R
Save as...	Ctrl+S
Print...	Ctrl+P
Cast...	
Translate to English	
View page source	Ctrl+U
Inspect	Ctrl+Shift+I

Elements   Console   Sources

```
<!DOCTYPE html>
<html lang="en">
 ▼ <head>
    <meta charset="UTF-8">
    <title>Getting Started In PHP</title>
  </head>
 ▼ <body>
    <h1>Hello World!</h1>
  </body>
</html>
```

html   body   h1

Styles   Computed   Layout   Event Listeners   DOM Breakpoints   Properties   »

Filter   :hov .cls +, ◁|

Don't forget

Note that the PHP **echo**
instruction literally
writes the entire content
contained within the
pair of ' ' single quote
marks. The examples in
this book demonstrate
embedded PHP script but
do not repeatedly list the
HTML code.

Scripting by the rules

Tag rules

When the PHP engine receives input from the web server it reads the input, from top to bottom, in a process called "parsing". During the parsing process, the PHP engine (a.k.a. parser) looks for the opening and closing **<?php** and **?>** tags and understands that the content between those tags is script code that it must interpret. Everything outside the **<?php** and **?>** tags is completely ignored, which allows PHP files to have mixed content and allows PHP code to be embedded within HTML, like this:

```
<p>Ignored by PHP and displayed by the browser</p>

<?php echo 'Script code that will be parsed' ; ?>

<p>Also ignored by PHP and displayed by the browser</p>
```

Hot tip

Typically, your embedded PHP code will always have opening and closing **<?php** and **?>** tags around script.

In order for this to work properly it is therefore important that all your PHP script code is enclosed between opening and closing **<?php** and **?>** tags, when embedded in an HTML file.

The only exception to this rule is when PHP script is written in a pure PHP file, which contains only code. In this case, it is preferable to omit the closing **?>** tag, like this:

```
<?php  echo 'Print this First' ;
       echo 'Print this Last' ;
```

Where your PHP script code intends only to insert a single string of text into an HTML document, you may optionally use the PHP short echo **<?=** and **?>** tags:

<?= 'Hello!' ; ?> is equivalent to **<?php echo 'Hello!' ; ?>**

Advanced PHP script code can also insert text only when a tested condition is met, like this:

```
<?php if ( $expression == true ) : ?>

       Insert this text only if the expression is true.

<?php else : ?>

       Otherwise insert this text.

<?php endif ; ?>
```

Don't forget

Conditional testing is fully explained and demonstrated later in this book, in Chapter 3.

18

Statement rules

Each statement within the PHP language must be terminated by a ; semicolon character – just as each sentence in the English language must be terminated by a . period character. The semicolon is recognized by the parser as marking the end of an individual instruction that it must interpret. So a PHP code block containing two statements could look like this:

```php
<?php echo 'First statement' ; echo 'Second statement' ; ?>
```

The closing ?> tag of a block of PHP code automatically implies a semicolon, however, so you can optionally omit the semicolon terminating the last statement of a PHP block, like this:

```php
<?php echo 'First statement' ; echo 'Second statement' ?>
```

Hot tip

It does no harm to terminate the last statement of a PHP block if you wish to do so.

Comment rules

It is often worthwhile adding comments to your PHP script code so it can be more easily understood by others, or by yourself when revisiting your code later. All whitespace and comments are completely ignored by the PHP parser so you can add as many comments as you like, without any adverse effect on performance.

Single-line comments may begin with a # hash character, or alternatively they may begin with a // double-slash sequence.

Multi-line (block) comments must be enclosed within /* and */ character sequences, as used in the C programming language:

```php
<?php
        echo 'First statement' ; // A single-line comment.

        /* This is a multi-line comment
        containing two lines of comment. */

        echo 'Second statement' ;

    echo 'Final statement' ; # Another single-line comment.

?>
```

Hot tip

The // single-line comment style is also used in C++ programming and the # single-line comment style is also used in Unix/Linux BASH shell scripting.

19

Improving performance

It is useful to understand that the PHP engine performs a sequence of operations in order to execute your PHP code:

PHP Code

Lex

Tokens

Parse

Abstract Syntax Tree

Compile

OPcode

Execute & Output

- **Lexing** – analyzes the code and generates a series of "tokens". For example, the tag **<?php** generates the token **T_OPEN_TAG**, the keyword **echo** generates the token **T_ECHO** and the string "Hello World!" generates **T_CONSTANT_ENCAPSED_STRING**.

- **Parsing** – arranges the tokens into an "Abstract Syntax Tree" (AST). This represents what operations should be performed. For example, the AST to print the result of adding two numbers might look something like this:

```
operation => ECHO,
operand => expression (
        operation => ADD,
        operand1 => 4,
        operand2 => 8
)
```

- **Compiling** – translates the Abstract Syntax Tree into instructional operation code ("OPcode"). This is an Intermediate Representation (IR) in machine language.

- **Executing** – runs the OPcode on the "Zend Virtual Machine" (VM). This interprets the OPcode to produce output.

Performing all these steps each time to execute a PHP script is not very efficient, so PHP includes an extension named "OPcache" that can be enabled to improve performance. OPcache stores OPcodes in memory so that lexing, parsing and compiling will only be performed when the PHP script is first executed. Subsequently, the low-level Intermediate Representation stored in memory can be executed on the Zend VM immediately.

To enable OPcache you will need to edit PHP's initialization file. The PHP installation folder, such as **C:\PHP**, contains files named **php.ini-development** and **php.ini-production**, which are initialization template files. When starting, PHP tries to find and load an initialization file named **php.ini**. A copy of either of the template files can be used for this purpose but the template named **php.ini-production** is recommended as the default settings in that file are optimized for performance and security. The OPcache extension is a file named **php_opcache.dll** located in an "ext" folder within the PHP installation folder.

1 Navigate to your PHP installation folder then save a copy of the **php.ini-production** file precisely as "php.ini"

2 Next, open the **php.ini** file in a text editor such as Windows' Notepad app

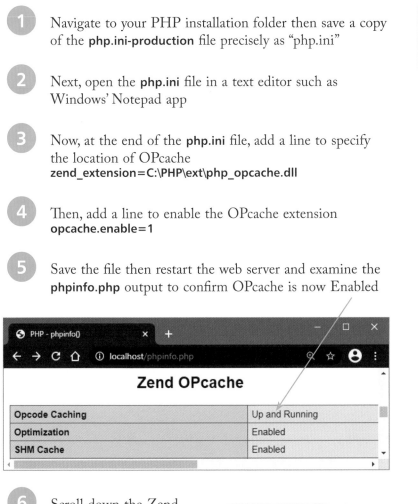

php.ini

3 Now, at the end of the **php.ini** file, add a line to specify the location of OPcache
zend_extension=C:\PHP\ext\php_opcache.dll

4 Then, add a line to enable the OPcache extension
opcache.enable=1

5 Save the file then restart the web server and examine the **phpinfo.php** output to confirm OPcache is now Enabled

PHP - phpinfo()	
← → C ⌂ ① localhost/phpinfo.php	

Zend OPcache

Opcode Caching	Up and Running
Optimization	Enabled
SHM Cache	Enabled

6 Scroll down the Zend OPcache section to see that "Cache hits" and "Cache misses" are both initially zero

7 Load the **hello.php** file and re-examine the **phpinfo.php** output repeatedly to see that "Cache misses" first increases to 1 then "Cache hits" increments on successive occasions

PHP Code

Enabling JIT compilation

The OPcache extension, described on pages 20-21, allows PHP to avoid repeated lexing, parsing, and compiling, but a further performance improvement can be made using "Just In Time" (JIT) compilation.

PHP's JIT compilation feature generates low-level CPU instructions in Assembly language code that can be executed by many different CPU types. It transforms the OPcode into architecture-specific machine code that can be executed directly by the system's CPU.

When PHP code is first run, the OPcode being executed by the Zend VM is examined by PHP to decide what would benefit from JIT compilation. Subsequent execution is performed directly by the system's CPU – bypassing the Zend VM.

Just In Time compilation is a great new feature introduced in PHP 8.

The OPcache extension must first be enabled to use JIT compilation, and you must specify in the PHP initialization file **php.ini** how much memory to allocate for compiled code.

...cont'd

1 Open the **php.ini** file in a text editor such as Windows' Notepad app

php.ini

2 Now, at the end of the **php.ini** file, add a line to specify memory allocation of 100 megabytes for compiled code **opcache.jit_buffer_size=100M**

3 Save the file then restart the web server and examine the **phpinfo.php** output to confirm JIT compilation is **On**

It is anticipated that performance will become more important in the future for CPU-intensive tasks such as Artificial Intelligence (AI). To compare the performance improvements provided by OPcache and JIT compilation, a benchmark PHP script might contain a variety of CPU-intensive tasks. Not listed here but included in the source code archive for this book is a PHP benchmark script that produced the results below when executed with various PHP configurations:

bench.php

OPcache Not Enabled

(2.3 Seconds)

With OPcache Enabled

(1.8 Seconds)

With OPcache Enabled & JIT Compilation On

(0.22 Seconds)

Summary

- PHP is a scripting language that is especially suited for web development as it can be embedded in HTML.

- PHP code is executed server-side on The Cloud, unlike JavaScript code that is executed client-side in the browser.

- A web server will first call upon the PHP engine to process PHP code before sending the response to the web browser.

- A local development environment can be created by installing a web server and the PHP engine on your own computer.

- The **http://localhost** URL is an alias for the numerical IP address of **http://127.0.0.1**.

- Access to the Abyss Web Server Console requires your user name and password, and is found at **http://localhost:9999**.

- The Web Server must be configured to recognize scripts so it will direct them to the PHP engine, by setting Interface, Interpreter, and Associated Extension parameters.

- The PHP code instruction **phpinfo()** can be used to serve up a web page containing your PHP version information.

- The PHP **echo** instruction literally writes the text content contained within following quote marks.

- All embedded PHP code must be enclosed within **<?php** and **?>** tags so it can be recognized by the PHP engine.

- Each statement within the PHP language must be terminated by a ; semicolon character.

- Single-line comments may begin with a **#** hash character or with a **//** double-slash sequence.

- Multi-line block comments must be enclosed within /* and */ character sequences.

- OPcache stores OPcodes in memory for execution by the Zend Virtual Machine.

- Just In Time compilation generates low-level instructions for execution directly by the system's CPU.

2 Storing values

This chapter demonstrates the various PHP containers in which data can be stored.

26 Creating variables

28 Quoting strings

30 Producing arrays

32 Sorting arrays

34 Describing dimensions

36 Checking types

38 Defining constants

40 Exploring superglobals

42 Summary

Creating variables

A "variable" is a named container in a PHP script in which a data value can be stored. The stored value can be referenced using the variable's name and changed (varied) as the script proceeds. The script author can choose any name for a variable providing it adheres to these three naming conventions:

- Names must begin with a $ dollar sign – for example, **$name**.

- Names can comprise letters, numbers and underscore characters, but not spaces – for example, **$subtotal_1**.

- The first character after the $ dollar sign must be a letter or an underscore character – it cannot be a number.

Note that variable names in PHP are case-sensitive, so **$name**, **$Name** and **$NAME** are three separate individual variables.

PHP variables are "loosely typed" meaning they can contain data of any type, unlike "strongly typed" variables in some languages, where the data type must be specified when the variable is created. So a PHP variable may happily contain an integer number, or a floating-point number, or a string of text characters, or a Boolean value of **TRUE** or **FALSE**, or an object, or a **NULL** empty value.

A variable is created in a PHP script simply by stating its name. The variable can then be assigned an initial value (initialized) by using the = assignment operator to state its value. This statement, and all others in PHP, must end with a semi-colon, like this:

$body_temp = 98.6 ;

The value contained within the variable can then be displayed by referencing it using the variable name, like this:

echo $body_temp ;

Usefully, the variable's value can be displayed as part of a mixed string by enclosing the string and variable name in <u>double quotes</u>:

echo "Body temperature is $body_temp degrees Fahrenheit" ;

The double quotes ensure that PHP will evaluate the whole string and substitute named variables with their stored values. This feature does not work if the string is enclosed in single quotes!

In PHP **$this** is a special variable so you cannot use "this" as a variable name.

Variables that are accessible throughout the script must have unique names. See page 82 for more on "variable scope".

Do not confuse the purpose of double and single quotes. Remember that PHP only makes variable substitutions for mixed strings enclosed within double quotes.

1 Create a valid HTML document, like the one listed on page 16, then insert PHP tags into the body section

```php
<?php
    # Statements to be inserted here.
?>
```

variable.php

2 Now, insert between the PHP tags a statement to create and initialize a variable

```php
$body_temp = 98.6 ;
```

3 Next, insert a statement to display the variable value alone

```php
echo $body_temp ;
```

Hot tip

4 Then, insert a statement to display the variable value substituted in a mixed string – assigned in double quotes

```php
echo "<p>Body temperature is $body_temp
                    degrees Fahrenheit " ;
```

Notice that variables created in the main body of a script, like the one in this example, are accessible "globally" – throughout the entire PHP script.

5 Insert a statement to assign a new value to the variable

```php
$body_temp = 37.0 ;
```

27

6 Finally, insert a statement to display the new variable value substituted in a mixed string

```php
echo "( $body_temp degrees Celsius )</p>" ;
```

Don't forget

7 Save the document in your web server's **/htdocs** directory as **variable.php** then open the page via HTTP to see the variable values get displayed

Each statement in the PHP language must be terminated by a semi-colon – just as each statement in the English language must be terminated by a period.

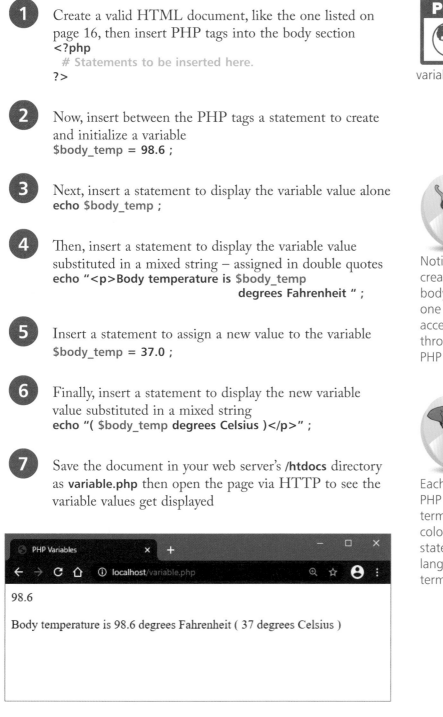

98.6

Body temperature is 98.6 degrees Fahrenheit (37 degrees Celsius)

Quoting strings

A "string" of text can be stored in a variable in much the same way as a numeric value, but the assignment must surround the string with quote marks to denote its beginning and end. Both single and double quote marks can be used for this purpose, but you must use the same type of quote marks to denote the beginning and end of the text string. For example, both these statements make valid string assignments:

$song_title = "Summertime Blues" ;

$song_title = 'Summertime Blues' ;

Where you wish to store a string of text that itself includes quote marks, you can "escape" the included quote marks by preceding them with a \ backslash character, or use the alternative type of quote mark within the string. For example, both these statements assign strings that include quote marks:

$song_title = "the \"Summertime\" aria by George Gershwin" ;

$song_title = 'the "Summertime" aria by George Gershwin' ;

The second technique, using double quote marks within the string, is easier to read and is preferred throughout this book.

String values can be displayed as part of a mixed string by enclosing the mixed string in <u>double quotes,</u> like this:

echo "Many regard $song_title as a popular classic" ;

The double quotes ensure that PHP will evaluate the mixed string and substitute named variables with their stored values. This feature does not work if the string is enclosed in single quotes!

String values can be joined together ("concatenated") into a single string using the . concatenation operator, like this:

```
$hi = 'Hello' ;
$bye = 'Goodbye' ;
$song_title = $hi . $bye ;        # 'HelloGoodbye'
```

Additionally, spaces and punctuation can usefully be inserted when concatenating strings, so the title assignment above could be modified to include a comma and a space:

$song_title = $hi . ', ' . $bye ;   # 'Hello, Goodbye'

28

Variable names cannot contain spaces – but the underscore character is often used in their place.

1 Create a valid HTML document, like the one listed on page 16, then insert PHP tags into the body section
```
<?php
    # Statements to be inserted here.
?>
```

string.php

2 Now, insert between the PHP tags a statement to create and initialize two variables
```
$phrase = 'The truth is rarely pure' ;
$author = 'Oscar Wilde' ;
```

3 Next, insert a statement to display a variable value alone
```
echo $phrase ;
```

4 Then, insert a statement to display the variable value substituted in a mixed string – assigned in double quotes
```
echo "<p>It is often said that <q>$phrase</q> </p>" ;
```

5 Insert a statement to concatenate a string to a variable
```
$phrase = $phrase . ' and never simple' ;
```

6 Finally, insert a statement to display both current variable values substituted in a mixed string
```
echo "<p><q>$phrase</q><cite>$author</cite></p>" ;
```

7 Save the document in your web server's **/htdocs** directory as **string.php** then open the page via HTTP to see the variable values get displayed

Hot tip

You can also use a shorthand concatenate assignment operator **.=** to join two strings – so that **$a = $a . $b** can be simply written as **$a .= $b**.

Hot tip

Adopt a consistent naming style for your variables – such as all lowercase **$my_var**, or "camelcase" **$myVar**.

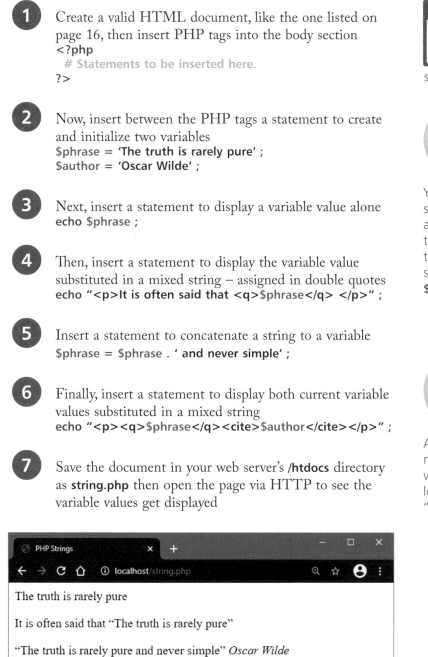

The truth is rarely pure

It is often said that "The truth is rarely pure"

"The truth is rarely pure and never simple" *Oscar Wilde*

Producing arrays

Indexed arrays

An array variable can store multiple items of data in sequential array "elements" that are numbered ("indexed") starting at zero. So, the first array value is stored in array element number zero. Individual array element values can be referenced using the variable name followed by the index number in square brackets. For example, **$days[0]** references the value stored in the first array element of an array variable named "days". Similarly, **$days[1]** references the value stored in the second array element, and so on. Variable arrays can be created by making multiple statements that assign values to successive elements, or by making a single statement using a PHP **array()** function to fill the elements:

$days[] = 'Monday' ; $days[] = 'Tuesday' ; $days[] = 'Wednesday' ;
or...
$days = array('Monday' , 'Tuesday' , 'Wednesday') ;
Both create an array where the value stored in each element can be referenced using its index number, such as **$days[0]**.

Square brackets denote "element" so are not needed after the variable name in the assignment using the **array()** function – they are only needed when addressing an element.

Associative arrays

When creating an array, you can optionally specify a key name for each element that can be used to reference that element's value:

$months['jan'] = 'January' ;
$months['feb'] = 'February' ;
$months['mar'] = 'March' ;

or...
$months =
array('jan' => 'January' , 'feb' => 'February' , 'mar' => 'March') ;
Both create an array where the value stored in each element can be referenced using its key name, such as **$months['jan']**.

Traversing arrays

All elements of an array can be traversed using a **foreach** loop to reference each element's value in turn and assign it to a variable:

```
foreach( $months as $value )
{
  # Use the current $value on each iteration.
}
```

The **foreach** construct exists specifically for arrays and provides an easy way to traverse all array element keys and values. See pages 66-71 for more on loops.

The keys can also be accessed on each iteration of the loop using
```
foreach( $months as $key => $value )
{
  # Use the current $key and $value on each iteration.
}
```

...cont'd

① Create a valid HTML document, like the one listed on page 16, then insert PHP tags into the body section
```php
<?php
    # Statements to be inserted here.
?>
```

array.php

② Now, insert between the PHP tags a statement to create and initialize a variable array with values
```php
$days = array( 'Monday' , 'Tuesday' , 'Wednesday' ) ;
```

You can set the first element key to 1, so the index will begin at 1 rather than 0, using
```php
$months = array( 1 => 'January' , 'February' , March' ) ;
```

③ Next, insert a statement to display the value in all array elements as a bulleted list
```php
foreach( $days as $value ) { echo "&bull; $value " ; }
```

④ Then, insert a statement to create and initialize a variable array with both keys and values
```php
$months = array( 'jan' => 'January' ,
                 'feb' => 'February' , 'mar' => 'March' ) ;
```

⑤ Finally, insert statements to display the key and value in all elements as a definition list
```php
echo '<dl>' ;
foreach( $months as $key => $value )
{ echo "<dt>$key<dd>$value" ; }
echo '</dl>' ;
```

If you specify key names you cannot reference elements by their index number, and if you specify the same key name twice, the second value will overwrite the first value.

⑥ Save the document in your web server's **/htdocs** directory as **array.php** then open the page via HTTP to see the variable array element values get displayed

You can easily create arrays containing sequential numbers or letters with the PHP **range()** function – for example, with
```php
$six = range( 1 , 6 ) ;
$a_z = range( 'a','z' ) ;
```

Sorting arrays

PHP provides two handy functions to convert between variable arrays and strings because they are so frequently used together. The **implode()** function converts an array to a string and inserts a specified separator between each value. Typically, this might be used to create a list of comma-separated values (csv), like this:

$csv_list = implode(' , ' , $array) ;

Conversely, the **explode()** function converts a string to an array by specifying a separator around which to break up the string. This might be used to create an array from a comma-separated list:

$array = explode(' , ' . $csv_list) ;

PHP also provides three useful functions to sort array elements into ascending alphanumeric order (a-z 1-9):

- **sort()** function – sorts by value discarding the original key.

- **asort()** function – sorts by value retaining the original key.

- **ksort()** function – sorts by key.

Existing array values are sorted with a simple statement, like this:

**$makers = array('Ford' , 'Chevrolet' , 'Dodge') ;
sort($makers) ;**

Array elements can also be sorted into descending alphanumeric order (9-1 z-a) with three similar functions:

- **rsort()** function – sorts by value discarding the original key.

- **arsort()** function – sorts by value retaining the original key.

- **krsort()** function – sorts by key.

It is important to recognize that specified key names will be discarded by the **sort()** and **rsort()** functions, so these should only be used where the key/value relationship is not significant – otherwise use the **asort()** and **arsort()** functions to retain the keys.

You can test if a variable is an array using the **is_array()** function – for example, **is_array($var) ;**

...cont'd

1 Create a valid HTML document, like the one listed on page 16, then insert PHP tags into the body section
```php
<?php
    # Statements to be inserted here.
?>
```

sort.php

2 Now, insert between the PHP tags a statement to create and initialize a variable array with key names and values
```php
$cars = array( 'Dodge' => 'Viper' ,
        'Chevrolet' => 'Camaro' , 'Ford' => 'Mustang' ) ;
```

3 Next, insert statements to display all keys and values of the array as a bulleted list within a definition list
```php
echo '<dl><dt>Original Element Order :<dd>' ;
foreach( $cars as $key => $value )
{ echo ' &bull; ' , $key . ' ' . $value ; }
```

You can discover the number of elements in an array with a **count()** function – for example,
$num = count($array) ;

33

4 Then, insert statements to display the array sorted by value
```php
asort( $cars ) ;
echo '<dt>Sorted Into Value Order :<dd>' ;
foreach( $cars as $key => $value )
{ echo ' &bull; ' , $key . ' ' . $value ; }
```

5 Finally, insert statements to display the array sorted by key
```php
ksort( $cars ) ;
echo '<dt>Sorted Into Key Order :<dd>' ;
foreach( $cars as $key => $value )
{ echo ' &bull; ' , $key . ' ' . $value ; }
echo '</dl>' ;
```

Do not use the **sort()** or **rsort()** functions where the keys are important.

6 Save the document in your web server's **/htdocs** directory as **sort.php** then open the page via HTTP to see the sorted array values get displayed

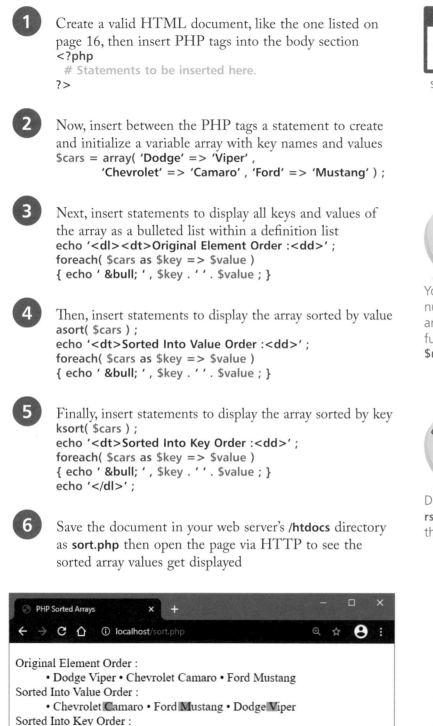

PHP Sorted Arrays

localhost/sort.php

Original Element Order :
  • Dodge Viper • Chevrolet Camaro • Ford Mustang
Sorted Into Value Order :
  • Chevrolet Camaro • Ford Mustang • Dodge Viper
Sorted Into Key Order :
  • Chevrolet Camaro • Dodge Viper • Ford Mustang

Describing dimensions

The numbering of array elements is more correctly known as the "array index" and, because element numbering starts at zero, is sometimes referred to as a "zero-based index". An array created with a single index is a one-dimensional array in which the elements appear in a single row:

Element content	A	B	C	D	E
Index numbers	[0]	[1]	[2]	[3]	[4]

Arrays can also have multiple indices – to represent multiple dimensions. An array created with two indices is a two-dimensional array in which the elements appear in multiple rows:

First index	[0]	A	B	C	D	E
	[1]	F	G	H	I	J
Second index		[0]	[1]	[2]	[3]	[4]

With multi-dimensional arrays, the value contained in each element is referenced by stating the number of each index. For example, with the two-dimensional array above, the element at [1][2] contains the letter H.

Two-dimensional arrays are useful to store grid-based information, such as XY coordinates. Creating a three-dimensional array, with three indices, would allow XYZ coordinates to be stored.

Creating a multi-dimensional array in PHP is simply a matter of creating an outer array, whose elements are themselves arrays. As usual, you may optionally specify a key name for each element – in this case to represent each inner array. Individual values can then be referenced using the key name and inner index number:

$matrix['Letter'][0]

It is, however, necessary to always enclose array variables that use quoted keys within curly braces when included in a string:

echo "Element value is {$matrix['Letter'][0]} " ;

All inner arrays in a multi-dimensional array can be accessed using a **foreach** loop to iterate through the arrays. A nested **foreach** loop can then reference each element in turn.

Beware

Multi-dimensional arrays with more than two indices can produce hard to read source code and may lead to errors.

...cont'd

1 Create a valid HTML document, like the one listed on page 16, then insert PHP tags into the body section
```php
<?php
    # Statements to be inserted here.
?>
```

matrix.php

2 Now, insert between the PHP tags a statement to create and initialize two regular variable arrays and a two-dimensional array with key names
```php
$letters = array( 'A' , 'B' , 'C' ) ;
$numbers = array( 1 , 2 , 3 ) ;
$matrix =
array( 'Letter' => $letters , 'Number' => $numbers ) ;
```

3 Next, insert a statement to display a single stored value
```php
echo "<p>Start : {$matrix['Letter'][0]} </p>" ;
```

4 Finally, insert statements to display the key and value in all elements as two unordered lists
```php
foreach( $matrix as $array => $list )
{
  echo '<ul>' ;
  foreach( $list as $key => $value )
  { echo "<li>$array [ $key ] = $value " ; }
  echo '</ul>' ;
}
```

5 Save the document in your web server's **/htdocs** directory as **matrix.php** then open the page via HTTP to see the variable array values get displayed

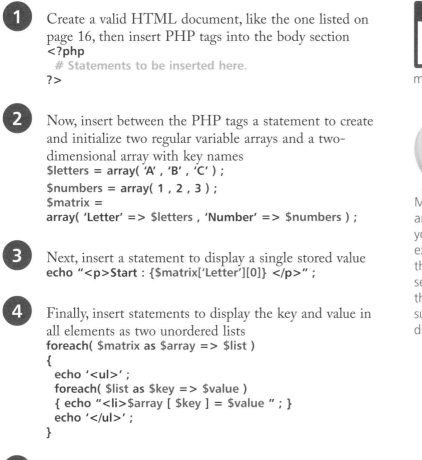

PHP Matrix   localhost/matrix.php

Start : A

- Letter [0] = A
- Letter [1] = B
- Letter [2] = C

- Number [0] = 1
- Number [1] = 2
- Number [2] = 3

Hot tip

Multi-dimensional arrays are more common than you might think. For example, an HTML form that allows multiple selections for inputs with the same name that are submitted as a multi-dimensional array.

Don't forget

Array variables that use quoted keys must be enclosed within curly braces when included in a string.

Checking types

PHP variables can store various types of data so it is useful to clearly understand each data type in detail:

- **string** – a series of characters in which each character is the size of one byte, up to a maximum length of 2GB. Strings enclosed in single quotes are treated as literals, whereas strings in double quotes will interpret special characters.

- **int** – a non-decimal number between 2,147,483,648 and -2,147,483,647, specified as a decimal (10-based), hexadecimal (16-based – prefixed with 0x), or octal (8-based – prefixed with 0).

- **float** – a floating-point decimal number or a number in exponential format. A float is also known as a "double".

- **bool** – an expression of a Boolean truth value, which may be only true or false.

- **array** – an ordered map of multiple data values that associates keys to values. The keys are index numbered by default or may be explicitly-specified labels.

- **object** – a class containing stored data properties and providing methods to process data.

- **resource** – a reference to an external resource that is created and used by special functions.

- **NULL** – a variable with no value whatsoever. It may have not been initialized, have been assigned the **NULL** constant, or have been nullified by the PHP **unset()** function.

The data type of any item can be checked by specifying it as the argument to the **gettype()** function. For example, where a variable **$num** contains an integer value, **gettype($num)** will return "integer", and where a variable **$str** contains a string value, **gettype($str)** will return "string", and so on. Where the data type cannot be identified, the **gettype()** function will return "unknown type".

Perhaps more usefully, the **var_dump()** function can check an item's data type and will dump structured information that displays its type and value.

Hot tip

The creation and use of PHP class objects are demonstrated fully in Chapter 7.

...cont'd

1 Create a valid HTML document, like the one listed on page 16, then insert PHP tags into the body section
```php
<?php
  # Statements to be inserted here.
?>
```

types.php

Hot tip

The creation and use of PHP filestream resources are demonstrated fully in Chapter 8.

2 Next, insert between the PHP tags a statement to create a filestream resource and an array
```php
$filestream = fopen( 'index.html' , 'r' ) ;
$data = array( 'PHP' , 1 , 2.3 , TRUE , NULL , array() ,
                    new Directory , $filestream ) ;
```

3 Now, insert a statement to display the data type stored within each array element
```php
foreach( $data as $type )
{
  var_dump( $type ) ;
  echo '<br> ' ;
}
```

4 Finally, insert statements to destroy the filestream resource then attempt to get its data type once more
```php
fclose( $filestream ) ;
echo gettype( $filestream ) ;
```

5 Save the document in your web server's **/htdocs** directory as **types.php** then open the page via HTTP to see the data types and values get displayed

Hot tip

The Boolean constants **TRUE** and **FALSE** are not case-sensitive, so may be written as **true** and **false**.

1000000

Hot tip

When creating a variable, always consider whether its value will ever change – if it will not, you should create a constant instead; for example, **define('PI' , 3.14) ;**

Defining constants

Fixed data values that will never change in a script should be stored in a PHP "constant", rather than in a variable. A constant is a named container in which numeric or string values can be stored and can be referenced using the constant's name.

Unlike a variable, a constant cannot contain Boolean values of **TRUE** or **FALSE**, nor represent an object, nor a **NULL** empty value. Additionally, a constant cannot be changed as the script proceeds. This safeguards the constant value from accidental alteration and is good programming practice.

Constant names are subject to the same naming conventions as variables, but it is traditional to use uppercase characters for constant names – to easily distinguish them from variable names. Constants are created using a **define()** function to specify the constant's name and the value it will contain, like this:

define('NAME' , value) ;

Most significantly, constant names are <u>not</u> prefixed by a $ dollar sign, so they cannot be included in mixed strings for display – as PHP cannot distinguish a constant name from a regular capitalized string. Consider these statements, for example:

define('USER' , 'Mike') ;
echo "Hello USER"

...the output here is **Hello USER**, not **Hello Mike** as desired.

In order to include a constant's value in an output string it must be referenced separately and "concatenated" to the string with the PHP . concatenation operator, like this:

echo 'Hello ' . USER ;

...the output here is now **Hello Mike** as desired.

Array constants, in which all elements contain fixed data values, can also be created using the **define()** function, like this:

define('WEEKDAYS' , ['Mon', 'Tue' , 'Wed' , 'Thu' , 'Fri']) ;

Constants defined by the script author can be used just like the predefined constants that are built into PHP, such as **PHP_VERSION** and **PHP_OS** that describe the version and server operating system.

1 Create a valid HTML document, like the one listed on page 16, then insert PHP tags into the body section
```
<?php
    # Statements to be inserted here.
?>
```

constant.php

2 Now, insert between the PHP tags a statement to create and initialize a constant
```
define( 'USER' , 'Mike' ) ;
```

3 Add a statement to create and initialize an array constant
```
define( 'PETS' , [ 'Kitten' , 'Puppy' , 'Hamster' ] ) ;
```

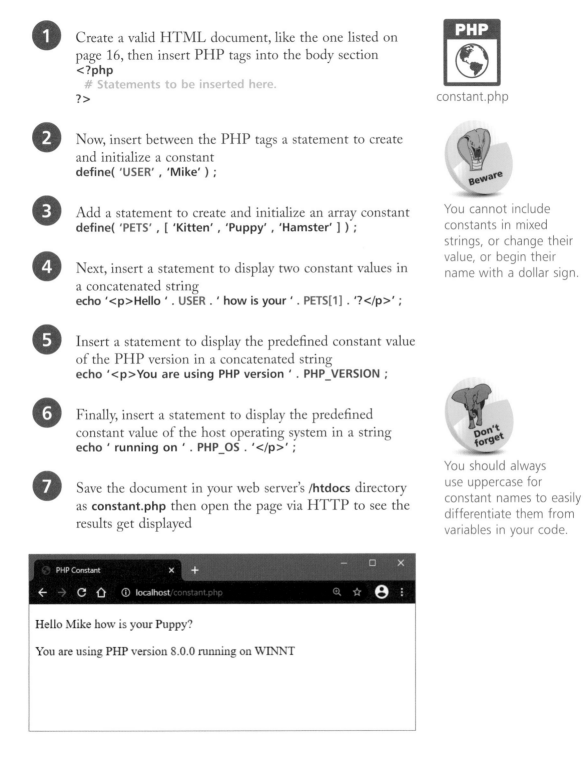

Beware

You cannot include constants in mixed strings, or change their value, or begin their name with a dollar sign.

4 Next, insert a statement to display two constant values in a concatenated string
```
echo '<p>Hello ' . USER . ' how is your ' . PETS[1] . '?</p>' ;
```

5 Insert a statement to display the predefined constant value of the PHP version in a concatenated string
```
echo '<p>You are using PHP version ' . PHP_VERSION ;
```

6 Finally, insert a statement to display the predefined constant value of the host operating system in a string
```
echo ' running on ' . PHP_OS . '</p>' ;
```

7 Save the document in your web server's **/htdocs** directory as **constant.php** then open the page via HTTP to see the results get displayed

Don't forget

You should always use uppercase for constant names to easily differentiate them from variables in your code.

PHP Constant — localhost/constant.php

Hello Mike how is your Puppy?

You are using PHP version 8.0.0 running on WINNT

Exploring superglobals

PHP provides several predefined variables that are always globally available anywhere within any script. These are aptly known as "superglobals" and are described briefly here:

- **$GLOBALS** – an associative array containing references to all variables that are currently defined in the global scope of the script, according to context. The variable names are the keys of this associative array – for example:
foreach($GLOBALS as $key => $var) echo "• $key ";

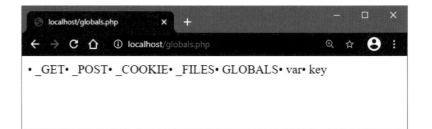

- **$_SERVER** – an array containing information such as headers, paths and script locations that is arbitrarily provided by the web server.

- **$_GET** – an associative array of variables passed to the script by appended URL parameters.

- **$_POST** – an associative array of variables passed to the script by the HTTP POST method.

- **$_FILES** – an associative array of uploaded file items passed to the script by the HTTP POST method.

- **$_COOKIE** – an associative array of variables passed to the script via HTTP from cookies on the user's computer.

- **$_SESSION** – an associative array containing variables available to each script on a website until the user exits.

- **$_REQUEST** – an associative array that by default contains the contents of **$_GET, $_POST** and **$_COOKIE**.

- **$_ENV** – an associative array of variables passed to the current script by the shell environment under which the PHP parser is running. Different systems will run different kinds of shells.

The **$_FILES** superglobal is used by the file upload example on page 152.

The **$_POST** superglobal is used by the HTML form submission example on page 138.

The **$_COOKIE** superglobal is used by the example on page 162 to get data from a cookie on the user's computer.

The **$_SESSION** superglobal is used by the example on page 167 to store data on the web server.

1 Create a valid HTML document, like the one listed on page 16, then insert PHP tags into the body section
```php
<?php
    # Statements to be inserted here.
?>
```

supers.php

2 Now, insert between the PHP tags a statement to display your server software details
```php
echo 'Web Server : '.$_SERVER[ 'SERVER_SOFTWARE' ].'<br>' ;
```

3 Add a statement to display this script name
```php
echo 'This Script : '.$_SERVER[ 'PHP_SELF' ].'<br>' ;
```

4 Next, insert statements to display the host name and the page request method
```php
echo 'Host Name : '.$_SERVER[ 'HTTP_HOST' ].'<br>' ;
echo 'Request Method : '.$_SERVER[ 'REQUEST_METHOD' ] ;
```

$_SERVER['PHP_SELF'] is used by the example on page 150 to create a "sticky" HTML form.

5 Insert a statement to display appended URL parameters
```php
foreach( $_GET as $key => $value )
{ echo '<hr>HTTP GET : '.$key.'='.$value ; }
```

$_SERVER['REQUEST_METHOD'] is used by the example on page 148 to establish whether an HTML form has been submitted by a user.

6 Save the document in your web server's **/htdocs** directory as **supers.php**

7 Open the page via HTTP by appending parameters to the script name in the browser address field, such as **?name=mike&lang=PHP**, to see them pass to the script

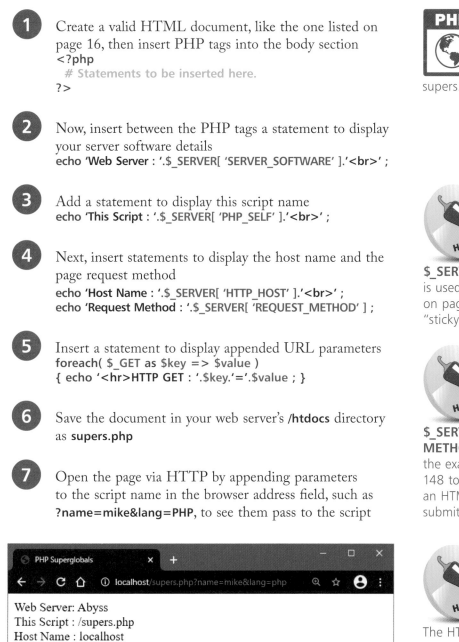

Web Server: Abyss
This Script : /supers.php
Host Name : localhost
Request Method : GET

HTTP GET : name=mike

HTTP GET : lang=php

The HTTP **GET** method is used by the example on page 182 to set parameters for an XML Web Service response.

41

Summary

- A variable is a named container in which changeable data can be stored.
- The value stored in a variable can be referenced using that variable's name.
- Variable names must begin with a $ dollar sign, may comprise letters, numbers and underscore characters, and the first character after the $ must only be a letter or an underscore.
- A variable can store an integer number, floating-point number, text string, Boolean value, object, or **NULL** value.
- A variable is initialized using the = assignment operator to assign an initial value to that variable.
- A variable's value can be displayed as part of a mixed string by enclosing the string and variable name in double quotes only.
- Strings may be enclosed in either single quotes or double quotes, and inner quote marks can be escaped using a backslash.
- String values can be joined together into a single string using the . concatenation operator.
- An array variable can store multiple items of data in sequential array elements that are numbered starting at zero by default.
- Optionally, key names may be specified for each array element.
- A **foreach** loop can traverse each element in an array.
- The **implode()** and **explode()** functions convert between strings and arrays by adding or removing specified separators.
- Arrays can be sorted into alphanumeric order by value or key.
- A multi-dimensional array is simply an array whose element values are themselves arrays.
- The **gettype()** and **var_dump()** functions can be used to check data types.
- A constant is a named container in which a fixed integer, floating-point number, or text string can be stored.
- Constant names are not prefixed by a $ and are all uppercase.
- A constant is initialized using the **define()** function.
- Superglobal variables are always globally available anywhere within any script.

3 Performing operations

This chapter demonstrates the various PHP operators for arithmetic, comparison and logical evaluation.

44 Doing arithmetic

46 Making comparisons

48 Examining conditions

50 Assessing logic

52 Comparing bits

54 Changing values

55 Grasping precedence

56 Summary

Doing arithmetic

The arithmetic operators commonly used in PHP scripts are listed in the table below, together with the operation they perform:

Operator	Operation
+	Addition
-	Subtraction
*	Multiplication
/	Division
%	Modulus
**	Exponentiation

Operators for addition, subtraction, multiplication and division act as you would expect. Care must be taken, however, to group expressions for clarity where more than one operator is used:

```
a = b * c - d % e / f ;          # This is unclear.

a = ( b * c ) - ( ( d % e ) / f ) ;   # This is clearer.
```

The **%** modulus operator divides the first given number by the second given number and returns the remainder of the operation. This is useful to determine if a number has an odd or even value.

The ****** exponentiation operator gives the result of raising the first operand to the power of the second operand.

```
a ** b          # Result of raising a to the b'th power.
```

Shorthand expressions can usefully be created by combining an arithmetic operator with the = assignment operator – for example:

```
a += b ;        # Equivalent to a = ( a + b ) ;
a -= b ;        # Equivalent to a = ( a - b ) ;
a *= b ;        # Equivalent to a = ( a * b ) ;
a /= b ;        # Equivalent to a = ( a / b ) ;
```

1 Create a valid HTML document, like the one listed on page 16, then insert PHP tags into the body section

```
<?php
  # Statements to be inserted here.
?>
```

arithmetic.php

2 Now, insert statements between the PHP tags to create and initialize two variables

```
$a = 5 ;
$b = 2 ;
```

3 Next, insert statements to display the results of simple arithmetical operations using the variable values

```
$result = $a + $b ; echo "Addition : $result <br>" ;
$result = $a - $b ; echo "Subtraction : $result <br>" ;
$result = $a * $b ; echo "Multiplication : $result <br>" ;
$result = $a / $b ; echo "Division : $result <br>" ;
```

4 Finally, insert a statement to display the results of arithmetical evaluations of the variable values

```
$result = $a % $b ; echo "Modulus : $result <br>" ;
$result = $a ** $b ; echo "Exponentiation : $result" ;
```

5 Save the document in your web server's **/htdocs** directory as **arithmetic.php** then open the page via HTTP to see the results and variable values get displayed

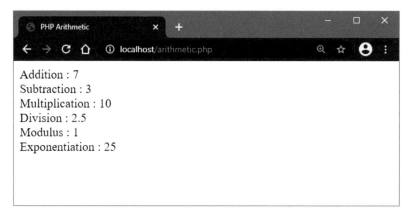

PHP has some useful functions to work with numbers. For example, **round($a)** rounds **$a** to the nearest integer and **number_format($a)** adds commas to **$a** denoting groups of thousands.

45

Making comparisons

The operators that are commonly used in PHP scripts to compare two values are listed in the table below:

Operator	Comparative test
==	Equality
===	Identicality
!==	Non-identicality
!= <>	Inequality
>	Greater than
<	Less than
>=	Greater than or equal to
<=	Less than or equal to
<=>	Spaceship

Hot tip

Equality and inequality operators are useful in testing the state of two variables to perform conditional branching in a PHP script.

The == equality operator compares two operands and returns a Boolean **TRUE** result if both are numerically equal in value, otherwise it returns **FALSE**. Characters and strings are also compared numerically by their ASCII code value. Conversely, the != inequality operator returns **TRUE** if the two operands are <u>not</u> equal, otherwise it returns **FALSE**.

The > "greater than" operator compares two operands and returns **TRUE** if the first is greater in value than the second, or it returns **FALSE** if it is equal or less in value. The < "less than" operator makes the same comparison but returns **TRUE** if the first operand is less in value than the second, otherwise it returns **FALSE**. Adding the = operator after a > "greater than" or < "less than" operator makes it also return **TRUE** when the two operands are exactly equal.

The <=> spaceship operator returns an integer value of 1 when the first operand is greater than the second, -1 when the first operand is less than the second, or 0 when the operands are equal.

The PHP **var_dump()** function can be used to see the type and value resulting from each kind of comparison.

…cont'd

① Create a valid HTML document, like the one listed on page 16, then insert PHP tags into the body section
```php
<?php
  # Statements to be inserted here.
?>
```

comparison.php

② Now, insert statements between the PHP tags to create and initialize five variables
```php
$zero = 0 ; $nil = 0 ; $one = 1 ; $upr = 'A' ; $lwr = 'a' ;
```

③ Next, insert statements to display equality comparisons
```php
echo "0 == 0 : " ;        var_dump( $zero == $nil ) ;
echo "<br>0 == 1 : " ;   var_dump( $zero == $one ) ;
echo "<br>A == a : " ;   var_dump( $upr == $lwr ) ;
echo "<br>A != a : " ;   var_dump( $upr != $lwr ) ;
```

④ Insert statements to display comparison evaluations
```php
echo "<hr>1 > 0 : " ;     var_dump( $one > $nil ) ;
echo "<br>0 >= 0 : " ;   var_dump( $zero >= $nil ) ;
echo "<br>1 <= 0 : " ;   var_dump( $one <= $nil ) ;
echo "<hr>1 <=> 0 : " ; var_dump( $one <=> $nil ) ;
echo "<br>1 <=> 1 : " ; var_dump( $one <=> $one ) ;
echo "<br>0 <=> 1 : " ; var_dump( $nil <=> $one ) ;
```

Hot tip

The ASCII code value for uppercase **'A'** is 65 and for lowercase **'a'** it's 97 – so their comparison here returns **FALSE**.

⑤ Save the document in your web server's **/htdocs** directory as **comparison.php** then open the page via HTTP to see the results get displayed

```
PHP Comparison        ×    +                    —  □  ×
←  →  C  ⌂   ① localhost/comparison.php        ⊕  ☆  ⊖  ⋮

0 == 0 : bool(true)
0 == 1 : bool(false)
A == a : bool(false)
A != a : bool(true)
─────────────────────────────────
1 > 0 : bool(true)
0 >= 0 : bool(true)
1 <= 0 : bool(false)
─────────────────────────────────
1 <=> 0 : int(1)
1 <=> 1 : int(0)
0 <=> 1 : int(-1)
```

Hot tip

A Boolean **TRUE** value is represented numerically by 1 in PHP language.

47

Examining conditions

Conditional operator

The conditional operator **?:** is also known as the "ternary" operator as it has three components. This operator first evaluates an expression for a **TRUE** or **FALSE** Boolean value, then returns one of two specified results depending on the evaluation. The conditional operator syntax looks like this:

(*test-expression*) ? *result-if-true* : *result-if-false* ;

The conditional operator can be used to evaluate whether a given number is one or more, to ensure correct grammar in output regarding singular and plural items. This avoids awkward phrases such as "There is 5":

$verb = ($number == 1) ? 'is' : 'are';
echo "There $verb $number" ;

In this case, when the **$number** variable has a value of one, the **'is'** result will be assigned to the **$verb** variable, otherwise the **'are'** result will be assigned.

The conditional operator can also be used to evaluate whether a given number is odd or even ("parity") by examining if there is any remainder after dividing the number by two, then assigning an appropriate string result, like this:

$parity = ($number % 2 == 0) ? 'Odd' : 'Even' ;
echo "$number is $parity" ;

In this case, when the modulus operation returns a value of one, the **'Odd'** result will be assigned to the **$parity** variable, otherwise the **'Even'** result will be assigned.

Null coalescing operator

PHP has a special **NULL** value that is a built-in constant, which represents a variable with no value whatsoever – not even zero. Variables that have not been assigned a value will evaluate as **NULL**. The snappily named **??** "null coalescing" operator can be used to traverse a number of operands, from left to right, and return the value of the first operand that is not **NULL**. If none of the operands have a value (and are not **NULL**) then the null coalescing operator will itself return a **NULL** result.

Beware

Do not use more than one **?:** conditional operator in a single statement as the results may be unpredictable.

1 Create a valid HTML document, like the one listed on page 16, then insert PHP tags into the body section
```php
<?php
  # Statements to be inserted here.
?>
```

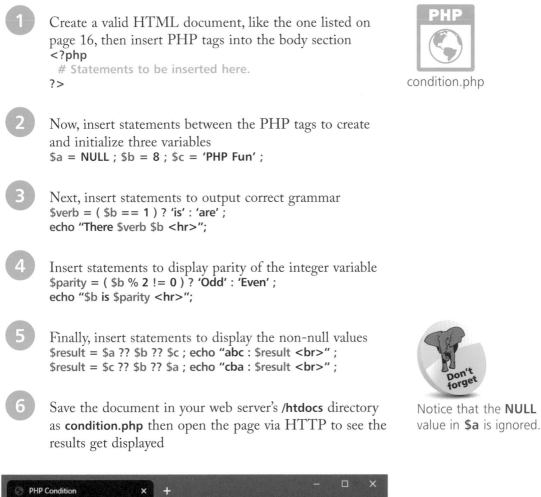

condition.php

2 Now, insert statements between the PHP tags to create and initialize three variables
```php
$a = NULL ; $b = 8 ; $c = 'PHP Fun' ;
```

3 Next, insert statements to output correct grammar
```php
$verb = ( $b == 1 ) ? 'is' : 'are' ;
echo "There $verb $b <hr>";
```

4 Insert statements to display parity of the integer variable
```php
$parity = ( $b % 2 != 0 ) ? 'Odd' : 'Even' ;
echo "$b is $parity <hr>";
```

5 Finally, insert statements to display the non-null values
```php
$result = $a ?? $b ?? $c ; echo "abc : $result <br>" ;
$result = $c ?? $b ?? $a ; echo "cba : $result <br>" ;
```

6 Save the document in your web server's **/htdocs** directory as **condition.php** then open the page via HTTP to see the results get displayed

Notice that the **NULL** value in **$a** is ignored.

49

Assessing logic

The logical operators most commonly used in PHP scripts are listed in the table below:

Operator		Operation
and	&&	Logical AND
or	||	Logical OR
xor		Logical eXclusive OR
!		Logical NOT

The logical operators are used with operands that have the Boolean values of **TRUE** or **FALSE**, or an expression that can convert to **TRUE** or **FALSE**.

The **and** operator will evaluate two operands and return **TRUE**, only if both operands are themselves **TRUE**. Otherwise, the **and** operator will return **FALSE**. This is used in conditional branching where the direction of a PHP script is determined by testing two conditions. If both conditions are satisfied, the script will go in a certain direction, otherwise it will take a different direction.

Unlike the **and** operator that needs both operands to be **TRUE**, the **or** operator will evaluate two operands and return **TRUE** if either one of the operands is itself **TRUE**. If neither operand is **TRUE** then the **or** operator will return **FALSE**. This is useful to perform an action if either one of two test conditions has been met.

The **xor** operator will evaluate two operands and only return **TRUE** if either one of the operands is itself **TRUE** – but not both. If neither operand is **TRUE**, or if both operands are **TRUE**, the **xor** operator will return **FALSE**.

The ! logical NOT operator is a "unary" operator – that is used before a single operand. It returns the inverse value of the given operand, so if the variable **$var** is a **TRUE** value then ! **$var** would return a **FALSE** value. The ! operator is useful to toggle the value of a variable in a loop with a statement like $var = ! $var. On each iteration the value is reversed, like flicking a switch on and off.

Hot tip

The **&&** operator is an alternative form of the **and** operator. Similarly, the **||** operator is an alternative form of the **or** operator.

Hot tip

The term "Boolean" refers to a system of logical thought developed by the English mathematician George Boole (1815-1864).

...cont'd

① Create a valid HTML document, like the one listed on page 16, then insert PHP tags into the body section
```php
<?php
    # Statements to be inserted here.
?>
```

logic.php

② Now, insert between the PHP tags statements to create and initialize two variables with Boolean values
```php
$yes = TRUE ; $no = FALSE ;
```

③ Next, insert statements to display AND evaluations
```php
$result = ( $no && $no ) ? 'TRUE' : 'FALSE' ;
        echo "No AND No returns $result <br>" ;
$result = ( $yes && $no ) ? 'TRUE' : 'FALSE' ;
        echo "Yes AND No returns : $result <br>" ;
$result = ( $yes && $yes ) ? 'TRUE' : 'FALSE' ;
        echo "Yes AND Yes returns $result <hr>" ;
```

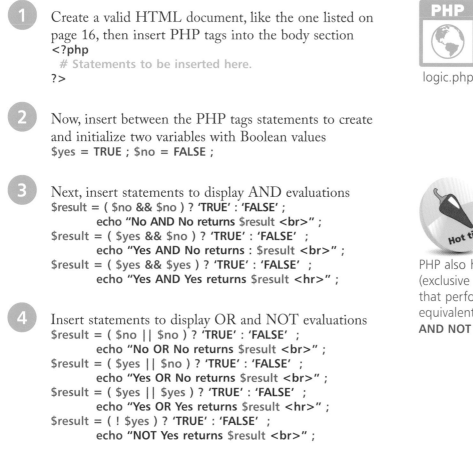

Hot tip

PHP also has an **XOR** (exclusive **OR**) operator that performs the equivalent evaluation of **AND NOT** together.

④ Insert statements to display OR and NOT evaluations
```php
$result = ( $no || $no ) ? 'TRUE' : 'FALSE' ;
        echo "No OR No returns $result <br>" ;
$result = ( $yes || $no ) ? 'TRUE' : 'FALSE' ;
        echo "Yes OR No returns $result <br>" ;
$result = ( $yes || $yes ) ? 'TRUE' : 'FALSE' ;
        echo "Yes OR Yes returns $result <hr>" ;
$result = ( ! $yes ) ? 'TRUE' : 'FALSE' ;
        echo "NOT Yes returns $result <br>" ;
```

⑤ Save the document in your web server's **/htdocs** directory as **logic.php** then open the page via HTTP to see the results get displayed

Don't forget

Notice that evaluation of **FALSE && FALSE** returns **FALSE** – maybe demonstrating the anecdote "two wrongs don't make a right".

Comparing bits

A byte comprises eight bits that can each contain a **1** or a **0** to store a binary number, representing decimal values from 0 to 255. Each bit contributes a decimal component only when that bit contains a **1**. Components are designated right-to-left from the "Least Significant Bit" (LSB) to the "Most Significant Bit" (MSB). The binary number in the bit pattern below represents decimal 50.

Bit No.	8 MSB	7	6	5	4	3	2	1 LSB
Decimal	128	64	32	16	8	4	2	1
Binary	0	0	1	1	0	0	1	0

It is possible to manipulate individual parts of a byte using "bitwise" operators. Bitwise operators allow evaluation and manipulation of specific bits within an integer.

Operator	Name	Binary number operation
|	OR	Return a **1** in each bit where either of two compared bits is a **1** Example: **1010 | 0101 = 1111**
&	AND	Return a **1** in each bit where both of two compared bits is a **1** Example: **1010 && 1100 = 1000**
~	NOT	Return a **1** in each bit where neither of two compared bits is a **1** Example: **~1010 = 0101**
^	XOR	Return a **1** in each bit where only one of two compared bits is a **1** Example: **1010 ^ 0100 = 1110**
<<	Shift left	Move each bit that is a **1** a specified number of bits to the left Example: **0010 << 2 = 1000**
>>	Shift right	Move each bit that is a **1** a specified number of bits to the right Example: **1000 >> 2 = 0010**

Hot tip

Each half of a byte is known as a "nibble" (4 bits). The binary numbers in the examples in the table describe values stored in a nibble.

Don't forget

Many PHP programmers never use bitwise operators, but it is useful to understand what they are and how they may be used.

52

Unless programming for a device with limited resources, there is seldom a need to utilize bitwise operators, but they can be useful. For instance, the ^ (eXclusive OR) operator lets you exchange values between two variables without the need for a third variable:

1 Create a valid HTML document, like the one listed on page 16, then insert PHP tags into the body section
```php
<?php
  # Statements to be inserted here.
?>
```

bitwise.php

2 Now, insert between the PHP tags statements to create and initialize two variables with integer values
```php
$x = 5 ; $y =10 ;
```

3 Next, add a statement to display the assigned values
```php
echo "X : $x , Y : $y <br>" ;
```

4 Insert three XOR statements to exchange the variable values by binary bit manipulation
```php
$x = $x ^ $y ;
$y = $x ^ $y ;
$x = $x ^ $y ;
```

Beware

5 Finally, add a statement to display the manipulated values
```php
echo "X : $x , Y : $y <br>" ;
```

Do not confuse bitwise operators with logical operators. Bitwise operators compare binary numbers, whereas logical operators evaluate Boolean values.

6 Save the document in your web server's **/htdocs** directory as **bitwise.php** then open the page via HTTP to see the XOR bitwise magic

Changing values

The PHP ++ increment operator and -- decrement operator alter the given number by 1 and return the resulting new value. These are most often used to count iterations in a loop. The increment operator increases the value by 1 and the decrement operator decreases the value by 1. Each of these operators may appear either before or after the variable containing the number to be changed – to different effect! When either of these operators is placed before the variable ("prefixed"), they change the value by 1 then return the modified value, but when they are placed after the variable ("postfixed") they return the current value, then change the value by 1:

change.php

1 Create a valid HTML document, like the one listed on page 16, then insert PHP tags into the body section
```
<?php
  # Statements to be inserted here.
?>
```

2 Now, insert between the PHP tags statements to create and initialize four variables with the same integer value
```
$a = $b = $c = $d = 5 ;
```

3 Next, add statements to change each of the values by 1 and display the new integers
```
echo "++A : ". ++$a . "<br>--B : ". --$b ."<hr>" ;
echo "C++ : ". $c++ . "[now C : ". $c ."]<br>" ;
echo "D-- : ". $d-- . "[now D : ". $d ."]<br>" ;
```

4 Save the document in your web server's **/htdocs** directory as **change.php** then open the page via HTTP to see the results

Hot tip

Notice how the **.** concatenation operator is used here to form strings. You can also use the **.=** concatenating assignment operator to append one string onto another string.

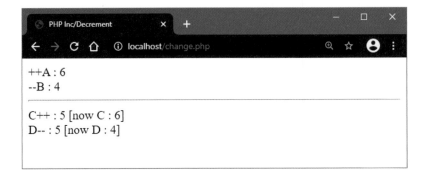

54

Grasping precedence

PHP operator precedence determines how expressions are grouped for evaluation. For example, the expression **1 + 5 * 3** evaluates to 16, not 18, because the * multiplication operator has a higher precedence than the **+** addition operator. Parentheses can be used to specify precedence, so that **(1 + 5) * 3** evaluates to 18. When operators have equal precedence, their "associativity" determines how expressions are grouped. For example, the - subtraction operator is left-associative, so **8 - 4 - 2** is grouped as **(8 - 4) - 2** and evaluates to 2. The table below lists common operators in order of precedence, with the highest-precedence ones at the top. Operators on the same line have equal precedence, so operator associativity determines how expressions are grouped.

Operator	Associativity	
**		Right
++ -- ~		Right
!		Right
* / %	Left	
+ - .	Left	
<< >>	Left	
< <= > >=		None
== != === !== <> <=>		None
&	Left	
^	Left	
|	Left	
&&	Left	
||	Left	
??		Right
?=	Left	
= += -= *= /= **= .= %= &= |= ^= <<= >>= =>		Right
and	Left	
xor	Left	
or	Left	
,	Left	

Beware

The eagle-eyed will notice that the alternative forms of logical operators have different levels of precedence. This can cause unexpected results in an expression such as **$bool = true and false** versus the alternative **$bool = true && false**. Try each of these then do **var_dump($bool)** to see the difference.

Summary

- Arithmetical operators can form expressions with operands for addition **+**, subtraction **-**, multiplication *****, division **/**, modulus **%**, and exponentiation ******.

- The assignment operator **=** can be combined with any arithmetical operator to perform an arithmetical calculation then assign the result.

- Comparison operators can form expressions with operands for equality **==**, inequality **!=**, identicality or not **===**, **!==**, greater **>**, less **<**, greater, less or equal **>=**, **<=**, **<=>**.

- The conditional operator **?:** evaluates an expression for a **TRUE** or **FALSE** Boolean value, then returns one of two specified results depending on the evaluation.

- The **??** null coalescing operator traverses operands from left to right and returns the first value that is not **null**.

- Logical operators **and**, **&&**, **or**, **||** and **xor** form expressions evaluating two operands and return a value of **TRUE** or **FALSE**.

- The logical **!** not operator returns the inverse Boolean value of a single operand.

- Bitwise operators **|**, **&**, **~**, **^**, **<<** and **>>** allow the evaluation and manipulation of specific bits within an integer.

- Increment **++** or decrement **--** operators that prefix a variable change its value by 1 and return the result.

- Increment **++** or decrement **--** operators that postfix a variable return its current value, then change its value by 1.

- Operator precedence determines how expressions are grouped for evaluation.

- When operators have equal precedence, their associativity determines how the expression is grouped for evaluation.

- The **var_dump()** function can be used to see the type and value resulting from an expression.

- The special **NULL** constant represents a variable that has no value whatsoever, not even zero.

4 Testing conditions

This chapter demonstrates the various PHP control structures that determine how a script will proceed.

58 **Seeking truth**

60 **Providing alternatives**

62 **Switching branches**

64 **Matching expressions**

66 **Performing loops**

68 **Looping while true**

70 **Breaking from loops**

72 **Summary**

Seeking truth

The **if** keyword is used to perform the basic conditional test that evaluates a given expression for a Boolean value of **TRUE** or **FALSE**. Statements within braces following the evaluation will only be executed when the expression is found to be **TRUE**. When the expression is found to be **FALSE**, the PHP parser simply moves on to the next part of the script.

The syntax of an **if** conditional test statement looks like this:

if (*test-expression*) { *statement-to-execute-when-true* ; }

There may be multiple statements to be executed when the test is **TRUE** but each statement must be terminated by a semi-colon:

```
if ( test-expression )
{
        statement-to-execute-when-true ;
        statement-to-execute-when-true ;
        statement-to-execute-when-true ;
}
```

Hot tip

The **if** construct is one of the most important features in PHP, and in most other programming languages.

Multiple expressions can be tested using the logical **&&** or **and** operator to ensure that following statements will only be executed when both expressions are found to be **TRUE**, like this:

```
if ( ( test-expression ) && ( test-expression ) )
{
        statement-to-execute-when-true ;
        statement-to-execute-when-true ;
        statement-to-execute-when-true ;
}
```

Alternatively, **if** conditional test statements can be nested to test multiple expressions so that statements will only be executed when all tests are found to be **TRUE**, like this:

```
if ( test-expression )
{
        if ( test-expression )
        {
                statement-to-execute-when-true ;
                statement-to-execute-when-true ;
                statement-to-execute-when-true ;
        }
}
```

Hot tip

When the code to be executed is just a single statement, the braces may optionally be omitted, but you may prefer to always include the braces for consistency.

Multiple **if** conditional test statements can be made to provide alternatives for the script to follow.

...cont'd

1 Between PHP tags, begin a script with a statement that initializes an integer variable
```php
<?php
$num = 8 ;
```

if.php

2 Next, add statements that output a result when a conditional test of numerical size is found to be **TRUE**
```php
if ( $num > 5 ) { echo "$num exceeds 5<br>" ; }
if ( $num <= 5 ) { echo "$num is below 6<br>" ; }
```

3 Now, add statements that output a result when a conditional test of parity is found to be **TRUE**
```php
if ( $num % 2 == 0 ) { echo "$num is Even<br>" ; }
if ( $num % 2 != 0 ) { echo "$num is Odd<br>" ; }
?>
```

4 Save the document in your web server's **/htdocs** directory as **if.php** then open the page via HTTP to see the results from successful tests get displayed

PHP Conditional If   localhost/if.php

```
8 exceeds 5
8 is Even
```

5 Edit the integer variable then save the modified script and refresh the browser to see the results from other successful tests get displayed
```php
$num = 3 ;
```

PHP Conditional If   localhost/if.php

```
3 is below 6
3 is Odd
```

When the tested condition is **FALSE**, the PHP parser ignores its statement block and simply moves on.

Providing alternatives

It is often preferable to extend an **if** statement by appending an **else** statement, specifying statements within braces to be executed when the expressions evaluated by the **if** statement are found to be **FALSE**, with this syntax:

```
if ( test-expression )
{
        statement-to-execute-when-true ;
        statement-to-execute-when-true ;
        statement-to-execute-when-true ;
}
else
{
        statement-to-execute-when-false ;
        statement-to-execute-when-false ;
        statement-to-execute-when-false ;
}
```

Alternative expressions may also be evaluated in a conditional test by adding an **elseif** statement, specifying statements within braces to be executed when the alternative expression is found to be **TRUE**. An **else** statement can be appended here too, to specify statements within braces to be executed when the expressions evaluated by the **if** and **elseif** statements are found to be **FALSE**, with this syntax:

```
if ( test-expression )
{
        statement-to-execute-when-true ;
        statement-to-execute-when-true ;
        statement-to-execute-when-true ;
}
elseif ( test-expression )
{
        statement-to-execute-when-true ;
        statement-to-execute-when-true ;
        statement-to-execute-when-true ;
}
else
{
        statement-to-execute-when-false ;
        statement-to-execute-when-false ;
        statement-to-execute-when-false ;
}
```

This is a fundamental programming technique that offers the script different directions in which to proceed, depending on the result of the evaluations, and is known as "conditional branching".

The **elseif** keyword can also be written as two separate words: **else if**.

You may come across some PHP scripts that use a **:** colon character rather than curly brackets. This is not recommended as **if** and **else if** will only be considered exactly the same when using curly brackets.

...cont'd

1 Between PHP tags, begin a script with a statement that outputs a result only when a tested expression is **TRUE**

```
<?php
if ( 4 > 2 ) { echo '<p>Yes, 4 is greater than 2 <br>' ; }
```

ifelse.php

2 Next, add a statement that outputs a result only when two tested expressions are both found to be **TRUE**

```
if ( ( 4 > 2 ) && ( 8 > 4 ) )
{ echo '4 is greater than 2 AND 8 is greater than 4<br>' ; }
```

3 Now, add a statement that outputs a result when a tested expression is found to be **TRUE** or **FALSE**

```
if ( 4 > 8 )
{ echo '4 is greater than 8 <br>' ; }
else
{ echo '4 is less than 8 <br>' ; }
```

4 Finally, add a statement that outputs a result when either of two tested expressions are found to be **TRUE** or when both tested expressions are found to be **FALSE**

```
if ( 4 > 8 )
{ echo 'This test is True </p>' ; }
elseif ( 8 > 4 )
{ echo 'Alternative test is True </p>' ; }
else
{ echo 'Both tests are False </p>' ; }
?>
```

Don't forget

You can nest conditional **if** tests (one inside another) so that statements in the inner block only get executed when both tests are found to be **TRUE**.

5 Save the document in your web server's **/htdocs** directory as **else.php** then open the page via HTTP to see the results of conditional branching get displayed

61

Switching branches

Conditional branching performed by multiple **if-elseif-else** statements can often be performed more efficiently by a **switch** statement when the test expression just evaluates one condition.

The **switch** statement works in an unusual way. It takes a given value as its parameter argument then seeks to match that value from a number of **case** statements. Code to be executed when a match is found is included in each **case** statement.

It is important to end each **case** statement with a **break** keyword statement, so the **switch** statement will then exit when a match is found without seeking further matches – unless that is the deliberate requirement.

Optionally, the list of **case** statements can be followed by a single final **default** statement to specify code to be executed in the event that no matches are found within any of the **case** statements. So the syntax of a switch statement typically looks like this:

Hot tip

It's always a good idea to include a **default** statement – even if it's only to output an error message when the **switch** statement fails.

```
switch ( test-value )
{
  case match-value : statements-to-execute-when-matched ; break ;
  case match-value : statements-to-execute-when-matched ; break ;
  case match-value : statements-to-execute-when-matched ; break ;
  default : statements-to-execute-when-no-match-found ;
}
```

A **switch** statement can have many **case** statements, but no two of its **case** statements can attempt to match the same value.

Where a number of match-values are to each execute the same statements, only the final **case** statement need include the statements to be executed and the **break** statement to exit the **switch** statement block. For example, to output the same message for match-values of 0, 1 and 2:

Don't forget

A **default** statement need not appear at the end of the **switch** block, but it is logical to place it there where it needs no **break** statement.

```
switch ( $number )
{
  case 0 :
  case 1 :
  case 2 : echo 'Less than 3' ; break ;
  case 3 : echo 'Exactly 3' ; break ;
  default : echo 'Greater than 3 or less than zero' ;
}
```

...cont'd

1 Between PHP tags, begin a script with statements that initialize two variables with an integer and character value

```php
<?php
$number = 2 ; $letter = 'B' ;
```

switch.php

2 Next, add a **switch** statement to match the integer value

```php
switch ( $number )
{
  case 1 : echo 'Number is One<br>' ; break ;
  case 2 : echo 'Number is Two<br>' ; break ;
  case 3 : echo 'Number is Three<br>' ; break ;
  default : echo 'Number is Unrecognized<br>' ;
}
```

3 Now, add a **switch** statement to match the character value

```php
switch ( $letter )
{
  case 'A' : echo 'Letter is A<br>' ; break ;
  case 'B' : echo 'Letter is B<br>' ; break ;
  case 'C' : echo 'Letter is C<br>' ; break ;
  default : echo 'Letter is Unrecognized<br>' ;
}
```

4 Finally, add a **switch** statement to match against multiple integer values

```php
switch ( $number )
{
  case 0 : case 1 : case 2 : echo 'Less than 3<br>' ; break ;
  default : echo '3 or more, or less than zero' ;
}
?>
```

Hot tip

In **switch** statements, the **case** keyword, match-value and colon character are regarded as a unique "label".

5 Save the document in your web server's **/htdocs** directory as **switch.php** then open the page via HTTP to see the results of conditional branching get displayed

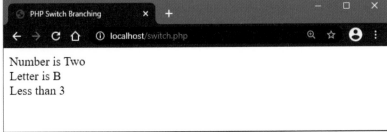

63

Matching expressions

Conditional branching can also be performed by **match** statements. These are an alternative to the **switch** statements, described on pages 62-63, and may often be a better choice.

Unlike a **switch** statement block, a **match** statement is a single expression that returns a value. It takes a given value as its parameter argument then seeks to match that value from a comma-separated list of alternatives enclosed within curly brackets. The value to be returned when a match is found is then specified after a **=>** fat arrow operator.

It is important to end each **match** statement with a ; semi-colon after the closing curly bracket to terminate the statement.

A **match** expression does not require any **break** statements so its code is significantly shorter than an equivalent **switch** block. The syntax of a **match** statement typically looks like this:

```
$result = match ( test-value )
{
  match-value => return-value ,
  match-value => return-value ,
  match-value => return-value ,
  default  => return-value ,
} ;
```

The **match** statement is a great new feature introduced in PHP 8.

Where a number of match-values are to each return the same value, they can be combined into a comma-separated single list. For example, to output the same message for match-values of 0, 1 and 2:

```
echo match ( $number )
{
  0 , 1 , 2 => 'Less than 3' ,
  3 => 'Exactly 3' ,
  default => 'Greater than 3 or less than zero' ,
} ;
```

It is useful to recognize that a **match** statement compares values for identicality, like using the === operator, whereas a **switch** statement compares values for equality, like using the == operator.

The steps in the example opposite use **match** statements to replicate the output from the previous **switch** statement example.

64

...cont'd

1 Between PHP tags, begin a script with statements that initialize two variables with an integer and character value

```php
<?php
$number = 2 ; $letter = 'B' ;
```

match.php

2 Next, add a **match** statement to match the integer value

```php
echo match ( $number )
{
  1 => 'Number is One<br>' ,
  2 => 'Number is Two<br>' ,
  3 => 'Number is Three<br>' ,
  default => 'Number is Unrecognized<br>' ,
} ;
```

3 Now, add a **match** statement to match the character value

```php
echo match ( $letter )
{
  'A' => 'Letter is A<br>' ,
  'B' => 'Letter is B<br>' ,
  'C' => 'Letter is C<br>' ,
  default => 'Letter is Unrecognized<br>' ,
} ;
```

4 Finally, add a **match** statement to match against multiple integer values

```php
echo match ( $number )
{
  0 , 1 , 2=> 'Less than 3<br>' ,
  default => '3 or more, or less than zero' ,
} ;
?>
```

5 Save the document in your web server's **/htdocs** directory as **match.php** then open the page via HTTP to see the results of conditional branching get displayed

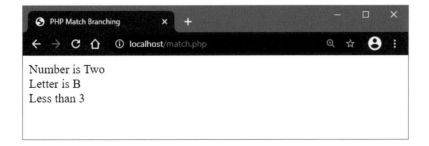

Hot tip

Compare the code in this example against the **switch** statements in the previous example to see the simplicity advantage of **match** statements.

65

Performing loops

A loop is a piece of code in a script that automatically repeats. One complete execution of all statements within a loop is called an "iteration", or a "pass". The length of a loop is controlled by a conditional test made within the loop. While the tested expression is found to be **TRUE** the loop will continue – until the tested expression is found to be **FALSE** at which point the loop ends.

In PHP there are four types of loop structure:

- **for** loop – performs a specified number of iterations.

- **while** loop – performs iterations only while a test made at the start of each iteration evaluates as **TRUE**.

- **do while** loop – performs iterations only while a test made at the end of each iteration evaluates as **TRUE**.

- **foreach** loop – performs iterations to traverse each element of an array, as introduced on page 30.

Perhaps the most interesting loop structure is the **for** loop, which typically has this syntax:

```
for ( initializer ; test-expression ; updater )
{
        statement-to-execute-when-true ;
        statement-to-execute-when-true ;
        statement-to-execute-when-true ;
}
```

The initializer is used to set a starting value for a counter of the number of iterations made by the loop. An integer variable is used for this purpose and is traditionally named "i".

Upon each iteration of the loop, the test-expression is evaluated and that iteration will only continue while this expression is **TRUE**. When the test-expression becomes **FALSE**, the loop ends immediately without executing the statements again. With every iteration the counter is updated then the statements executed.

Loops can be nested, one within another, to allow complete execution of all iterations of an inner nested loop on each iteration of the outer loop.

Hot tip

The updater may be an incrementer, or it may be a decrementer in a loop that counts down rather than counting up.

1 Between PHP tags, create a script with a **for** loop to output the loop counter value on each of three iterations

```php
<?php
for ( $i = 1 ; $i < 4 ; $i++ )
{
  echo "<dt>Outer loop iteration $i" ;

  # Nested loop to be inserted here.
}
?>
```

forloop.php

2 Save the document in your web server's **/htdocs** directory as **forloop.php** then open the page via HTTP to see the loop counter values get displayed

3 Now, insert a nested **for** loop to output its loop counter value in a list on each of three iterations

```php
for ( $j = 1 ; $j < 4 ; $j++ )
{
  echo "<dd>Inner loop iteration $j" ;
}
```

4 Save the document once more then open the page via HTTP to see both loop counter values get displayed

A **for** loop counter can also count down – by decrementing the counter value on each iteration using **$i--** in place of **$i++**.

Looping while true

A **while** loop is an alternative to the **for** loop described in the previous example. The **while** loop also requires an initializer, test-expression, and an updater, but these are not neatly listed within a single pair of parentheses as they are in a **for** loop. Instead, the initializer must appear before the start of the loop block, and the test-expression must appear within parentheses after the **while** keyword, followed by braces containing both an updater and the statements to be executed on each iteration.

```
initializer
while ( test-expression )
{
        statement/s-to-be-executed ;
        updater ;
}
```

A **do while** loop provides a subtle variation on the syntax above by placing the **do** keyword before the loop block and moving the **while** statement to after the loop block:

```
initializer
do {
        statement/s-to-be-executed ;
        updater ;
}
while ( test-expression ) ;
```

Beware

Ensure that the test expression in a loop structure will at some point become **FALSE** to avoid creating an infinite loop that never ends.

Both **while** loops and **do while** loops will proceed to make iterations until the test-expression is found to be **FALSE**, at which point the loop will exit. It is therefore essential that the loop body contains code that will, at some point, change the result of the test-expression evaluation – otherwise an infinite loop is created, which will lock the system. The significant difference between a **while** loop and a **do while** loop is that a **while** loop will not make a single iteration if the test-expression is **FALSE** on its first evaluation. In contrast, a **do while** loop will always make at least one iteration because its statements are executed before the evaluation is made. If this is desirable, a **do while** loop is obviously the best choice, otherwise the choice between a **for** loop and a **while** loop is largely a matter of personal preference. One rule of thumb suggests that a **for** loop is best used to perform a specific number of iterations, whereas a **while** loop is best used to iterate until a certain condition is met. Loops are the perfect partner to use with arrays as each iteration can effortlessly read or write into successive array elements.

...cont'd

1 Between PHP tags, begin a script with a statement to create an array

```php
<?php
$numbers = array( 10 , 20 , 30 ) ;
```

whileloop.php

2 Next, add a **while** loop to output the value of each array element

```php
echo '<dt>While Loop : ' ;
$i = 0 ;
while ( $i < 3 )
{
  echo "<dd>Element $i = $numbers[$i] " ;
  $i++ ;
}
```

3 Now, add a **do while** loop to output the value of each array element

```php
echo '<dt>Do While Loop : ' ;
$i = 0 ;
do
{
  echo "<dd>Element $i = $numbers[$i] " ;
  $i++ ;
}
while ( $i < 3 ) ;
?>
```

Change the value in this test expression to zero – so **while ($i = 0)** in both loops – to see only the first iteration of the **do while** loop get executed.

4 Save the document in your web server's **/htdocs** directory as **whileloop.php** then open the page via HTTP to see the array element values get identically displayed

Breaking from loops

The **break** keyword can be used to prematurely terminate a loop when a specified condition is met. The **break** statement is situated inside the loop statement block and is preceded by a test expression. When the test returns **TRUE**, the loop ends immediately and the program proceeds on to the next task. For example, in a nested inner loop the program proceeds to execute the next iteration of the outer loop.

breakcontinue.php

1 Between PHP tags, begin a script with a **for** loop that performs three iterations

```php
<?php
for ( $i = 1 ; $i < 4 ; $i++ )
{
    # Nested loop to be inserted here (Step 2).
}
```

2 Next, insert a nested **for** loop that also performs three iterations

```php
for ( $j = 1 ; $j < 4 ; $j++ )
{
    # Statements to be inserted here (Steps 5 & 6).
}
?>
```

3 Now, insert a statement that outputs the value of both loop counters on each iteration

```php
echo "Running i = $i and j = $j <br>" ;
```

4 Save the document in your web server's **/htdocs** directory as **breakcontinue.php** then open the page via HTTP to see both loop counter values get displayed

```
PHP Breaking Loops        ×   +                    □  ×
←  →  C  ⌂   ⓘ localhost/breakcontinue.php    ⊕  ☆  ⊖  ⋮

Running i = 1 and j = 1
Running i = 1 and j = 2
Running i = 1 and j = 3
Running i = 2 and j = 1
Running i = 2 and j = 2
Running i = 2 and j = 3
Running i = 3 and j = 1
Running i = 3 and j = 2
Running i = 3 and j = 3
```

5 Next, insert this **break** statement at the very beginning of the inner loop block, to break out of the inner loop – then save the document and view the change

```
if ( $i == 2 && $j == 1 )
{
  echo "Breaks inner loop when i = $i and j = $j <br>" ;
  break ;
}
```

Here, the **break** statement halts all three iterations of the inner loop when the outer loop tries to run it the second time.

The **continue** keyword can be used to skip a single iteration of a loop when a specified condition is met. The **continue** statement is situated inside the loop statement block and is preceded by a test expression. When the test returns **TRUE**, that single iteration ends.

6 Now, insert this **continue** statement at the beginning of the inner loop block, to skip the first iteration of the inner loop – then save the document and view the change

```
if ( $i == 1 && $j == 1 )
{
  echo "Continues inner loop when i = $i and j = $j <br>" ;
  continue ;
}
```

Here, the **continue** statement just skips the first iteration of the inner loop when the outer loop tries to run it for the first time.

Summary

- The **if** keyword performs the basic conditional test that evaluates an expression for a Boolean value of **TRUE** or **FALSE**.

- Statements within braces following the evaluation will only be executed when the expression is found **TRUE**.

- Multiple expressions can be tested using the logical **&&** operator, or by nesting multiple **if** conditional tests.

- The **else** keyword specifies statements to be executed when the expression evaluated by the **if** statement is found **FALSE**.

- The **elseif** keyword is used to append an alternative expression to be evaluated and statements to be executed when **TRUE**.

- Multiple **if-elseif-else** statements can often be performed more efficiently by a **switch** statement.

- Each **case** statement specifies a value to be matched in a **switch** statement block and must end with a **break** keyword.

- A **default** statement specifies code to be executed in the event that no matches are found within any **case** statements.

- A **match** statement is a single expression that returns a value when it finds a match to its specified parameter.

- A loop is a piece of code in a script that automatically repeats until a test expression becomes **FALSE**.

- The PHP loop structures are **for**, **while**, **do while** and **foreach**.

- A **for** loop structure specifies an initializer, a test expression and an updater that increments (or decrements) a counter.

- An updater must always be included in the statement block of a **while** loop and a **do while** loop.

- Unlike a **while** loop, a **do while** loop will always execute its statements at least once.

- The **break** keyword can be used to prematurely terminate a loop when a specified condition is met.

- The **continue** keyword can be used to skip a single iteration of a loop when a specified condition is met.

5 Employing functions

This chapter demonstrates how to create reusable blocks of code in functions.

74 Defining functions

76 Passing arguments

78 Varying parameters

80 Naming parameters

82 Recognizing scope

84 Returning values

86 Allowing union types

88 Calling back

90 Summary

Defining functions

PHP provides many built-in functions that can be called by name in your scripts to execute predefined actions, such as the array sorting functions described on page 32. Additionally, you may create your own custom functions to execute specified actions when called. This usefully allows PHP scripts to be modularized into sections of code that are easier to understand and maintain.

Your custom function names may contain any combination of letters, numbers and the underscore character, but must begin with a letter or an underscore. Understandably, to avoid conflict, the name may not duplicate an existing built-in function name so, for example, you may not create a custom function named "sort".

Unlike PHP variables, function names are case-insensitive so **cube()**, **Cube()** and **CUBE()** can all reference the same function. Nonetheless, it is recommended you always use the same case as that used to name the function in the function definition.

PHP variable names are case-sensitive, but PHP function names are not.

A function definition is created in a PHP script simply by stating its name after the **function** keyword, followed by parentheses and curly brackets (braces) containing the statements to be executed each time that function gets called:

```
function function_name ( )
{
    statement-to-be-executed ;
    statement-to-be-executed ;
    statement-to-be-executed ;
}
```

A PHP script can then call upon a defined function by name using *function_name*( )**; to execute the statements it contains whenever required. Although the interpreter runs the script from top to bottom, a function call can appear before the function definition. This is not good programming practice, however, so you should define functions before they are called.

Functions may contain any valid PHP script code and may even contain a further function definition. In that case, the inner function will not exist until the outer function has been called.

...cont'd

1 Begin a PHP script with a statement to define a function

```php
<?php
function greet()
{
  echo 'Hello User!<br>' ;
}
```

function.php

2 Next, add a statement to call the function defined in the previous step, to have it execute its statement

```php
greet() ;
```

3 Now, define another function that contains an inner function definition and a further statement

```php
function outer()
{
  function inner()
  {
    echo 'Inner function called.<br>' ;
  }
  echo 'Inner function created.<br>' ;
}
```

4 Finally, add statements to call each of the functions defined in the previous step

```php
outer() ;
inner() ;
?>
```

5 Save the document in your web server's **/htdocs** directory as **function.php** then open the page via HTTP to see the output from each function call

Hot tip

Remove the call to the outer function to see an undefined function error when the script attempts to call the inner function.

75

Passing arguments

Data can be passed to functions as "arguments" in the same way you can pass arguments to some built-in PHP functions. For example, the **sort()** function takes the array to be sorted as its argument. Functions can be created with any number of arguments but when called, data must be supplied for each argument to avoid an error.

A function accepting arguments is defined by including a comma-separated list of "parameters" within the parentheses after the function name, like this:

```
function function_name ( $arg_1 , $arg_2 , $arg_3 )
{
    statement-to-be-executed ;
    statement-to-be-executed ;
    statement-to-be-executed ;
}
```

Parameter names must adhere to the same naming conventions required for PHP variables and should ideally be meaningful, to represent the nature of the data that will be passed. The argument data must be passed by the call in the correct order and can then be used by the statements within that function.

Optionally, the function definition can specify the type of data to be passed from the caller by including a type description before the parameter name. Valid type descriptions include **int, float, string, bool, callable** and **array**. When types are specified, a call that attempts to pass an incorrect data type to the function will result in an error.

It is important to recognize that by default, argument data is passed "by value". This means that if a function call specifies a variable name, only a copy of the data within that variable gets passed to the function. Modifying the argument will not affect the original data stored in the variable when it is passed by value.

If you want a function to modify data stored in a variable, specified in a function call, you must pass it "by reference". This allows the function to operate directly on the original data. Modifying the argument will affect the original data in the variable when it is passed by reference. To ensure that an argument is always passed to a function by reference, you need simply prefix an **&** ampersand before the parameter name in the function definition.

Don't forget

Parameters must be specified in the function declaration as a comma-separated list, and argument values passed by the caller as a comma-separated list.

...cont'd

arguments.php

1 Begin a PHP script with a statement to initialize two variables with the same integer value
```
<?php
$a = $b = 5 ;
```

2 Next, define a function that accepts two integer arguments – one by value and the other by reference
```
function modify( int $val , int &$ref )
{
  // Statements to be inserted here.
}
```

3 Now, insert statements to output the passed values, then increment those values and display the modified values
```
echo "Passed values : $val , $ref<br>" ;
$val++ ;
$ref++ ;
echo "Incremented values : $val , $ref<hr>" ;
```

4 After the function block, add a statement to call the function, passing the variable values as arguments
```
modify( $a , $b ) ;
```

5 Finally, add a statement to display the values now stored in each variable
```
echo "Stored values : $a , $b" ;
?>
```

The **int** type description in this example specifies that only integer data values can be passed as arguments to the function.

6 Save the document in your web server's **/htdocs** directory as **arguments.php** then open the page via HTTP to see the argument and variable values

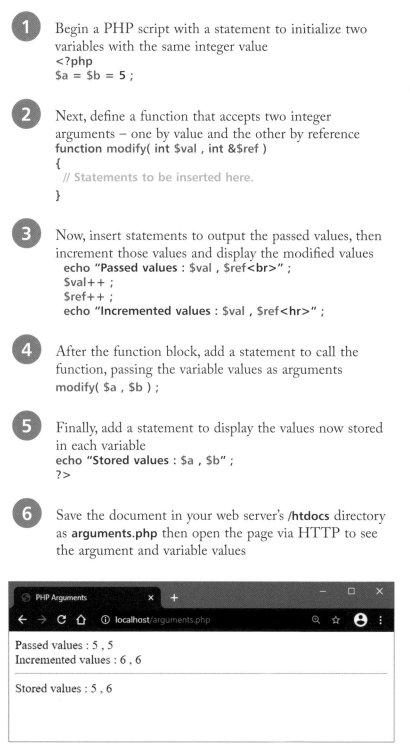

```
Passed values : 5 , 5
Incremented values : 6 , 6
────────────────────────
Stored values : 5 , 6
```

Varying parameters

Default argument values can optionally be specified in a function definition by assignment to the parameter name, like this:

```
function function_name ( $arg_1 , $arg_2 = "Default String" )
{
  statement-to-be-executed ;
  statement-to-be-executed ;
  statement-to-be-executed ;

}
```

This allows a function call to be made that specifies either one or two argument values. If only one argument is specified, it is assigned to the first parameter and the default value is used by the second parameter. Where default values are specified for parameters, they must only appear in the parameter list following (to the right of) parameters that have no specified default value. Otherwise, a call without the correct total number of arguments would cause an error.

Beware

If multiple default values are specified there is currently no way to skip a parameter in a function call, to assign an argument value to a particular parameter.

If you need to create a function that will accept an unknown number of arguments, PHP has a special … "splat" operator for that purpose. This can be used in a function definition, like this:

```
function function_name ( ...$args )
{
  statement-to-be-executed ;
  statement-to-be-executed ;
  statement-to-be-executed ;

}
```

When the … splat operator is used to prefix a parameter name in a function definition, multiple arguments can be passed to that parameter to create an array. The array can be traversed like any other array to manipulate the passed in argument values.

Hot tip

The … splat operator is also sometimes known as the "scatter" operator.

Additionally, the … splat operator can be used to "unpack" an array specified in a function call to pass its element values as individual arguments, like this:

```
function function_name ( $arg_1 , $arg_2 , $arg_3 )
{
  echo $arg_1 + $arg_2 + $arg_3 ;
}

$arr = [ 1 , 2 , 3 ] ;

function_name ( ...$arr ) ;          # Outputs 6
```

1 Begin a PHP script by defining a function that provides default string values to its two parameters

```php
<?php
function drink( string $tmp = 'hot' , string $flavor = 'tea' )
{
  // Statement to be inserted here.
}
```

parameters.php

2 Next, insert a statement to display its default values or passed in argument values

```php
  echo "Drinking $tmp $flavor.<br>" ;
```

3 After the function block, add function calls that optionally pass string arguments

```php
drink() ; drink( 'iced' ) ; drink( 'cold' , 'lemonade' ) ;
```

4 Now, define a function that can accept multiple integer arguments and display their total value

```php
function add( int ...$numbers )
{
  $total = 0 ;
  foreach( $numbers as $num ) { $total += $num ; }
  echo "<hr>Total : $total" ;
}
```

5 Finally, after the function block add a statement to call the function in the previous step and pass three values

```php
add( 1 , 2 , 3 ) ;
?>
```

6 Save the document in your web server's **/htdocs** directory as **parameters.php** then open the page via HTTP to see the argument and default values

Hot tip

You can specify regular positional parameters before a parameter that accepts multiple arguments with the ... splat operator. Only arguments that outnumber the positional elements will be added to the array of the final parameter.

79

PHP Parameters   localhost/parameters.php

Drinking hot tea.
Drinking iced tea.
Drinking cold lemonade.

Total : 6

Naming parameters

A function definition will typically include parameters that will require a caller to pass argument values to the function in the same order as the parameters are listed in the function definition. Consequently, these are known as "positional parameters".

PHP also supports "named parameters" that allow a caller to pass argument values to the function in any order. In this case, the call must specify each parameter name and argument value separated by a colon. The parameter name in the call is the parameter name specified in the function definition – but without the $ prefix.

```
function function_name ( $arg_1 , $arg_2 )
{
  echo $arg_1 + $arg_2 ;
}
```

```
function_name ( arg_1 : 'Hot' , arg_2 : 'Tea' ) ;   # Outputs Hot Tea
function_name ( arg_2 : 'Tea' , arg_1 : 'Hot' ) ;   # Outputs Hot Tea
```

When a function definition specifies a default value for a parameter, and the caller does not pass an argument value for that parameter, the default value will be used just as when calling positional parameters.

The use of named parameters can improve code readability and also allows a caller to pass argument values to specific parameters while assuming default values for other parameters. For example, given a function definition with two parameters that each have specified default values, a positional parameter call <u>cannot</u> specify an argument value for the second parameter alone. It can't skip the first parameter. A named parameter call, on the other hand, <u>can</u> specify an argument value for the second parameter and assume the default value for the first parameter.

```
function_name ( arg_2 : arg_value ) ;
```

You can use both named parameters and positional parameters in a function call but all positional parameters must appear before named parameters within the call. Using a positional parameter after a named parameter in a function call will create an error, as the PHP parser cannot correctly assign the argument value.

Additionally, the ... splat operator can be used in a function definition to collect parameter names and values from a named parameter call, and their names will be preserved.

Hot tip

Named parameters is a great new feature introduced in PHP 8.

...cont'd

1 Begin a PHP script by defining a function that provides default string values to its two parameters

```php
<?php
function cook( string $prep = 'fried' , string $food = 'rice' )
{
  echo "<li>Serving $prep $food" ;
}
```

named.php

2 Next, add statements to call the function with positional parameters and to call with named parameters

```php
cook( 'boiled' , 'egg' ) ;
cook( food : 'cheese' , prep : 'grilled' ) ;
```

3 Now, add calls to specify an argument value for the second parameter alone, and a call using one positional parameter and one named parameter

```php
cook( food : 'rice' ) ; cook( 'baked' , food :  'potato' ) ;
```

4 Then, define a function to collect named parameters and add a call to display passed names and values

```php
function register( ...$args )
{
  foreach( $args as $name => $value )
  { echo "<dt>".$name."<dd>".$value ; }
}
register( Topic : 'PHP' , Series : 'Programming' ) ;
?>
```

Don't forget

Named parameters require all non-optional parameters (those without a specified default value) to be passed an argument value, just as positional parameters do.

5 Save the document in your web server's **/htdocs** directory as **named.php** then open the page via HTTP to see the argument and default values

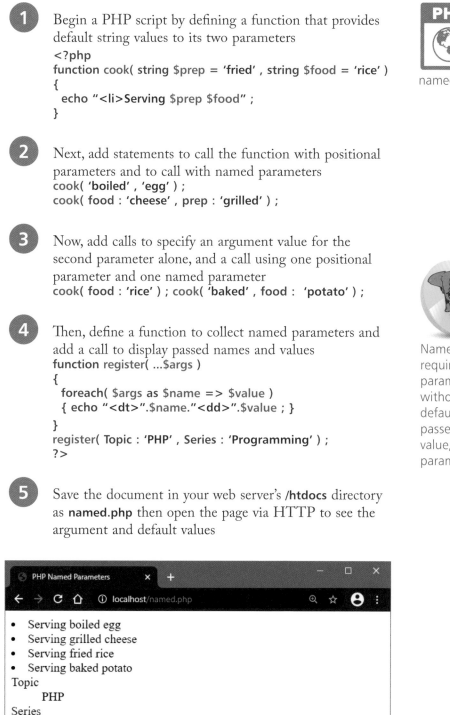

PHP Named Parameters

localhost/named.php

- Serving boiled egg
- Serving grilled cheese
- Serving fried rice
- Serving baked potato

Topic
> PHP

Series
> Programming

Global variables in PHP are not like those in other programming languages such as C, where they are automatically available to functions. In PHP, global variables can only be used in functions if first explicitly declared inside the function block using the **global** keyword.

Recognizing scope

When creating custom functions it is important to understand how variable accessibility is limited by the variable's "scope":

● Variables created outside a function have "global" scope, but are not normally accessible from within any function block.

● Variables created inside a function have "local" scope so are only accessible from within that particular function block.

As a variable created within a function is not accessible from elsewhere, its name may duplicate the name of a variable outside a function block, or within another function block, without conflict. This allows a global variable to contain a different value to a local variable of the same name.

If you wish to use a global variable inside a function, you must first include a statement with the **global** keyword to declare that the variable name refers to a global variable, like this:

global *variable-name* ;

The scope of a variable created within a function can be altered to make it available globally by preceding its declaration with the **global** keyword – but this is bad practice and should be avoided.

Function statements can call other functions to execute their statements and can also call themselves to execute recursively. As with loops, a recursive function must alter the state of a tested condition so it will not continue forever. This might be a counter value that gets passed in as an argument from an initial function call, then gets incremented on successive recursive calls until it exceeds a value specified in a test. Alternatively, a static local variable could be declared to store an incrementing value, like this:

static *variable-name* ;

Unlike other local variables, which lose their value when the program scope leaves the function, static variables retain their value. This means that the updated value of an incremented value stored in a static local variable is recognized on each function call.

A recursive function might otherwise reference a global variable counter value that gets incremented on successive recursive calls, until it exceeds a value specified in a test.

...cont'd

1 Begin a PHP script by initializing a global variable with an integer and displaying the variable value

```php
<?php
$number = 1 ; echo "Global number : $number<br>" ;
```

scope.php

2 Next, define and call a function that initializes a like-named local variable and displays that variable value

```php
function show_local()
{
  $number = 100 ; echo "Local number : $number<hr>" ;
}
show_local() ;
```

3 Now, define and call a recursive function that increments the global variable and a static variable on each call

```php
function recur()
{
  global $number ;        static $letter = 'A' ;
  if( $number < 14 )
  {
    echo "$number:$letter | " ;
    $number++ ; $letter++ ; recur() ;
  }
}
recur() ;
```

If you remove the **static** keyword from this function, the **$letter** variable will simply contain **'A'** each time the function is called.

4 Finally, after the function block add a statement to display the modified global variable value

```php
echo "<hr>Global number : $number" ;
?>
```

5 Save the document in your web server's **/htdocs** directory as **scope.php** then open the page via HTTP to see the global and local variable values

PHP also has a special **$GLOBALS** array in which the value of a global variable can be referenced by its name. In this example you could alternatively use **$GLOBALS['number']** to get the value.

Returning values

A custom PHP function can return a value to the caller by adding a statement using the **return** keyword, like this:

```
function function_name ( )
{
  statement-to-be-executed ;
  statement-to-be-executed ;
  return value ;
}
```

The **return** statement is optional and if omitted, functions will return a **NULL** value to the caller by default.

Functions can only return a single item to the caller, so they cannot return multiple values. You can, however, assign multiple values to elements of an array and have a function return the single array to the caller, then unpack the values.

A **return** statement can include an expression to be evaluated so its single result will be returned to the caller. For example:

```
function square( int $number )
{
  return $number * $number ;
}

echo square( 3 ) ;        # Outputs 9
```

To ensure a function will only return a value of a desired data type, the function declaration can, optionally, specify the return type description such as **int, float, string, bool** or **array**, like this:

```
function function_name ( ) : int
{
  statement-to-be-executed ;
  statement-to-be-executed ;
  return value ;
}
```

When a return data type is specified, a function that attempts to return an incorrect data type to the caller will result in an error.

...cont'd

return.php

① Begin a PHP script by defining a function that must only return an array of data

```
<?php
function supply() : array
{
  // Statement to be inserted here.
}
```

② Next, insert a statement to return an array of four mixed values

```
return array ( 75 , 3.142 , 'Super PHP' , True ) ;
```

③ After the function, add a statement that calls the function and assigns the returned array values to a variable

```
$array = supply() ;
```

④ Finally, add a loop to display each of the values returned from the function

```
foreach( $array as $data )
{
  echo "Element Value : $data<br>" ;
}
?>
```

⑤ Save the document in your web server's **/htdocs** directory as **return.php** then open the page via HTTP to see the returned values

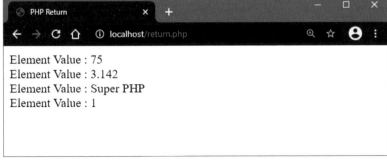

In PHP, the Boolean **TRUE** value is represented numerically as 1.

85

Allowing union types

It is generally preferable to restrict parameters to accept only one specific data type, but sometimes you may want a parameter to allow calls to pass values of different data types. This is possible by specifying the acceptable data types in the function definition as a "union type". This is pipe-separated list of PHP data types before the parameter name with this syntax:

function *function_name* (*type*|*type*|*type* $*arg*)

Similarly, multiple acceptable data types of the value returned from a function can be specified as a union type with a pipe-separated list in a function definition:

function *function_name* (*type*|*type* $*arg*) : *type*|*type*

Union types support all the PHP data types except for **void**, but does support the special **null** type. This means that a function can return a value of a specific data type or **null**. This is a fairly common requirement known as a "nullable union". It can be specified as a pipe-separated list or with a shorthand notation:

type*|null** or **?*type

The shorthand version can only be used with a single data type, not with a union type, and the **null** type can only be used as part of a union type.

PHP also has a **mixed** pseudo type that allows a parameter or return value to be of any type except for **void**. It is equivalent to a union type that looks like this:

string|int|float|bool|null|array|object|callable|resource

The **mixed** pseudo type cannot be used in union with other types because it already represents all acceptable types. When no data type is explicitly specified for a parameter, PHP assumes the type to be **mixed**. When no data type is explicitly specified for a function's return value, PHP assumes the type to be **mixed** or **void**.

Hot tip

Union types is a great new feature introduced in PHP 8.

Hot tip

The **callable** type is simply a type hint. It may be specified for a parameter that accepts a callable function.

...cont'd

1 Begin a PHP script by defining a function that can accept an integer or floating-point number as its argument, and can return either an integer or floating-point number

```php
<?php
function half( int|float $arg ) : int|float
{
    // Statements to be inserted here.
}
```

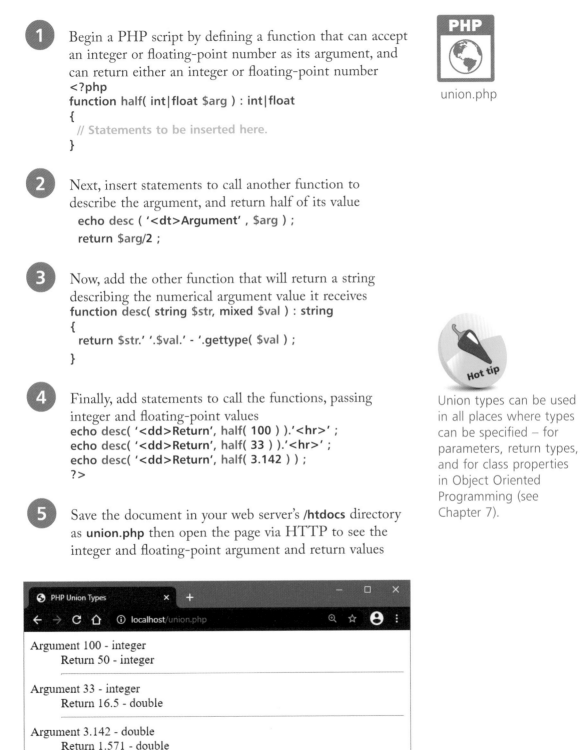

union.php

2 Next, insert statements to call another function to describe the argument, and return half of its value

```php
echo desc ( '<dt>Argument' , $arg ) ;
return $arg/2 ;
```

3 Now, add the other function that will return a string describing the numerical argument value it receives

```php
function desc( string $str, mixed $val ) : string
{
    return $str.' '.$val.' - '.gettype( $val ) ;
}
```

4 Finally, add statements to call the functions, passing integer and floating-point values

```php
echo desc( '<dd>Return', half( 100 ) ).'<hr>' ;
echo desc( '<dd>Return', half( 33 ) ).'<hr>' ;
echo desc( '<dd>Return', half( 3.142 ) ) ;
?>
```

Union types can be used in all places where types can be specified – for parameters, return types, and for class properties in Object Oriented Programming (see Chapter 7).

5 Save the document in your web server's **/htdocs** directory as **union.php** then open the page via HTTP to see the integer and floating-point argument and return values

PHP Union Types — localhost/union.php

Argument 100 - integer
   Return 50 - integer

Argument 33 - integer
   Return 16.5 - double

Argument 3.142 - double
   Return 1.571 - double

Beware

Don't forget to add a terminating ; semicolon after each anonymous function definition.

Calling back

PHP allows you to create "anonymous" functions that have no name specified in the function definition. Like other functions, these can accept arguments if parameters are specified and they can optionally return a value when called. Unlike other function definitions, which are code constructs, an anonymous function definition is an expression. This means that each anonymous function definition must be terminated by a semicolon, like this:

```
function ( )
{
  statement-to-be-executed ;
  statement-to-be-executed ;
  return value ;
} ;
```

On its own an anonymous function is of little use as, without a name, it cannot be called, but it can be useful in other ways:

- Assigned to a variable, an anonymous function can be called using the variable name.

- Passed as a callable argument to another function, an anonymous function can be called later as a "callback".

- Returned from a function, an anonymous function retains access to the returning function's variables in "closure".

By assigning an anonymous function to a variable you do, in effect, give the function a name and can call it and pass it arguments as you would any other function – using the variable name. Similarly, when you pass an anonymous function to another function it can be called back and passed arguments as you would any other function – using the parameter name. The PHP **use** keyword and **&** ampersand prefix allow an anonymous function to reference a local variable in the returning function.

callback.php

 Begin a PHP script by assigning to a variable an anonymous function that accepts a single argument
```
<?php
$hello = function ( $user ) { echo "Hello $user!<br>" ; } ;
```

2 Next, add a statement that calls the anonymous function and passes a single argument
```
$hello( 'Mike' ) ;
```

3 Now, define a regular function that accepts a single callable argument and calls that function passing a string

```php
function greet( callable $anon )
{
  $anon( 'Carole Anne' ) ;
}
```

4 Add a statement to call the function, defined in the previous step, passing the anonymous function that was assigned to a variable in the first step

```php
greet( $hello ) ;
```

5 Next, define another regular function that has one local variable and returns an anonymous function that references the local variable value

```php
function meet() : callable
{
  $time = 'morning' ;
  return function( $name ) use( &$time )
  { return "Good $time, $name!" ; } ;
}
```

Don't forget

Remember to include the & ampersand prefix to create a reference to the variable value.

6 Assign to a variable the function defined in the previous step then call that function, passing a string argument

```php
$meeting = meet() ;
echo $meeting( 'Susan' ) ;
?>
```

7 Save the document in your web server's **/htdocs** directory as **callback.php** then open the page via HTTP to see the returned values from anonymous functions

```
PHP Callback          ×   +          —   □   ×
←  →  C  ⌂  ⓘ localhost/callback.php      ⊕  ☆  😎  ⋮

Hello Mike!
Hello Carole Anne!
Good morning, Susan!
```

Hot tip

Notice that the final function call gets the **'morning'** string from the parent scope.

Summary

- Custom functions allow PHP scripts to be modularized into sections of code that are easier to understand and maintain.

- Function names must begin with a letter or underscore character and are not case-sensitive.

- A function is defined by stating its name after the **function** keyword, then parentheses and braces containing statements.

- A function accepting arguments is defined by including a comma-separated list of parameters within the parentheses.

- Optionally, a function definition can specify the type of data to be passed from the caller before the parameter name.

- Argument data is normally passed by value but can be passed by reference if the parameter name is given an **&** prefix.

- Default argument values can optionally be specified in a function definition by assignment to the parameter name.

- The ... splat operator allows multiple arguments to be passed to a parameter in order to create an array.

- Named parameters allow a caller to pass argument values to the function in any order.

- Variables created outside a function have global scope, but are not accessible from within a function block unless it includes a declaration using the **global** keyword.

- Variables created inside a function have local scope so are only accessible from within that particular function block.

- Local variables lose their value when the program scope leaves the function, but **static** variables retain their value.

- The **return** keyword returns a single item to the caller and the function definition can optionally specify the return data type.

- A union type is a pipe-separated list of PHP data types that allow various types of arguments and returns.

- The **use** keyword and **&** ampersand prefix allow an anonymous function to reference a local variable in the returning function.

6 Manipulating strings

This chapter demonstrates various ways to manipulate text strings in PHP scripts.

92 Comparing characters

94 Searching text

96 Extracting substrings

97 Changing case

98 Formatting strings

100 Making dates

102 Encoding entities

104 Summary

Comparing characters

PHP provides a number of built-in functions to perform a comparison of two text strings. The simple **strcmp()** function accepts two string arguments for comparison and will return one of three integer values depending on the result. When the strings exactly match, **strcmp()** will return zero. When the first string argument is greater than the second, **strcmp()** will return 1, but when the first string argument is less than the second, **strcmp()** will return -1.

The **strncmp()** function works in a similar way, but accepts a third integer argument to specify the number of characters from the start of the strings to be compared.

Strictly speaking, the **strcmp()** returned values will be a positive integer, zero, or a negative integer – but are typically values of 1, 0, or -1.

The **strcmp()** and **strncmp()** functions attach different importance to uppercase and lowercase characters when comparing strings. When you prefer to ignore case, you can use the alternative companion functions **strcasecmp()** and **strncasecmp()** instead.

To appreciate the results from each of the four comparison functions it is useful to understand how the comparisons are actually made. Each character has a standard numerical "ASCII" value where lowercase a-z is in the range 97-122 and uppercase A-Z is in the range 65-90. Comparing the first value in each range we see that "a" (97) is greater than "A" (65). Supplying these as arguments, the **strcmp()** function would therefore return 1, as the first argument is greater than the second. Conversely, if you specify "A" (65) as the first argument and "a" (97) as the second argument then the **strcmp()** function would return -1, as the first argument is less than the second. With string comparisons, each character is compared in sequence to ensure that strings containing the same characters in a different order are not seen to be incorrectly equal. For example, comparing "ABC" and "BAC" the first character "A" (65) is less than first character "B" (66) so the **strcmp()** function would return -1, as the first argument is less than the second.

ASCII is an abbreviation for the American Standard Code for Information Exchange that specifies the universal standard character coding scheme.

The ASCII value of any character can be found by specifying the character as an argument to the PHP **ord()** function, and the length of a string can be found by specifying it as the argument to the PHP **strlen()** function.

1 Begin a PHP script with statements to initialize four variables with string values

```php
<?php
$str1 = 'PHP in easy steps' ;
$str2 = 'PHP in easy steps' ;
$str3 = 'PHP In Easy Steps' ;
$str4 = 'php in easy steps' ;
```

characters.php

2 Next, add statements to compare the strings

```php
echo "'$str1' versus '$str2' : ".strcmp($str1, $str2).'<br>' ;
echo "'$str1' versus '$str3' : ".strcmp($str1, $str3).'<br>' ;
echo "'$str1' versus '$str4' : ".strcmp($str1, $str4).'<hr>' ;
```

3 Now, add a statement for a case-insensitive comparison

```php
echo 'Comparison Ignoring Case :<br>' ;
echo "'$str1' versus '$str4' : ".strcasecmp($str1, $str4) ;
```

4 Finally, add a loop to count and display the total ASCII code value of the first string

```php
$total = 0 ;
for ( $i = 0 ; $i < strlen( $str1 ) ; $i++ )
{
  $total += ord( $str1[ $i ] ) ;
}
echo "<hr>ASCII Total '$str1' : $total" ;
?>
```

5 Save the document in your web server's **/htdocs** directory as **characters.php** then open the page via HTTP to see the string comparisons

```
PHP Characters          ×   +                      —  □  ×
→  C  ⌂   ① localhost/characters.php        ⊕ ☆ 😀 :

'PHP in easy steps' versus 'PHP in easy steps' : 0
'PHP in easy steps' versus 'PHP In Easy Steps' : 1
'PHP in easy steps' versus 'php in easy steps' : -1
─────────────────────────────────────────────────
Comparison Ignoring Case :
'PHP in easy steps' versus 'php in easy steps' : 0
─────────────────────────────────────────────────
ASCII Total 'PHP in easy steps' : 1536
```

Don't forget

Character order is relevant as the ASCII totals for two differently ordered strings could be equal, but the strings would not match.

Searching text

PHP provides a number of built-in functions to search a string to find a specified substring or single character. The simple **strpos()** function accepts two arguments to specify the string in which to search, and the substring to find. It will search in sequence from the start of the string to find a match. When a match is found, the search halts and the **strpos()** function returns an integer, which is the character index number position within the string at which the first occurrence of a match begins. When no match is found, the **strpos()** function returns **FALSE**.

The **strrpos()** function works in a similar way but returns the index number position at which the first occurrence of a match begins when searching in reverse order, from the end of the string.

Other PHP search functions can return a part of the searched string, rather than an index number indicating a match position.

The **strstr()** function accepts two arguments to specify the string in which to search, and the substring to find. It will search from the start of the string to find a match. When a match is found, the search halts and the **strstr()** function returns the remainder of the searched string from where the first occurrence of a match begins. When no match is found, the **strstr()** function returns **NULL**.

Similarly, where character case is unimportant, you can use the companion **stristr()** function to make a case-insensitive search. This will return the remainder of the searched string from where the first occurrence of a case-insensitive match begins.

The **strchr()** function works in a similar way but accepts two arguments to specify the string in which to search, and a single character to find. The companion **strrchr()** function begins searching in reverse order, from the end of the string. Both return the remainder of the searched string from where the first occurrence of a match begins.

You can also seek a match by specifying the string to search and the substring to find as arguments to **str_contains()**, **str_starts_with()** and **str_ends_with()** functions. These each return a Boolean **TRUE** or **FALSE** value according to the search result. The return can assign an appropriate string to describe the result.

Beware

Notice that there is no **strrstr()** (companion function to **strstr()**) to search in reverse order.

Begin a PHP script with statements to initialize a variable with a string value, then report its length `<?php`
`$str = 'Most Users usually find PHP useful.' ;`
`echo "'$str'<br>String Length : ".strlen( $str ) ;`

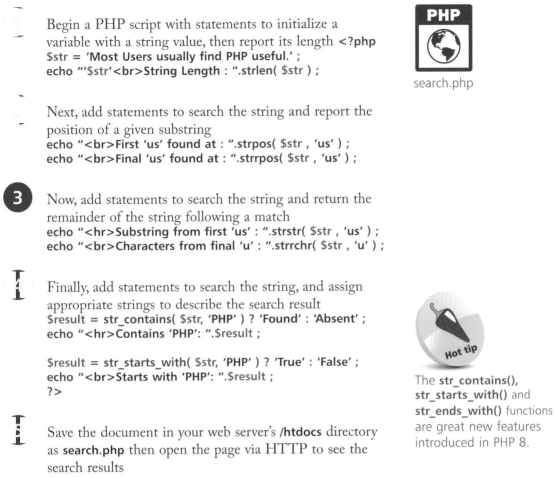

search.php

Next, add statements to search the string and report the position of a given substring
`echo "<br>First 'us' found at : ".strpos( $str , 'us' ) ;`
`echo "<br>Final 'us' found at : ".strrpos( $str , 'us' ) ;`

3 Now, add statements to search the string and return the remainder of the string following a match
`echo "<hr>Substring from first 'us' : ".strstr( $str , 'us' ) ;`
`echo "<br>Characters from final 'u' : ".strrchr( $str , 'u' ) ;`

Finally, add statements to search the string, and assign appropriate strings to describe the search result
`$result = str_contains( $str, 'PHP' ) ? 'Found' : 'Absent' ;`
`echo "<hr>Contains 'PHP': ".$result ;`

`$result = str_starts_with( $str, 'PHP' ) ? 'True' : 'False' ;`
`echo "<br>Starts with 'PHP': ".$result ;`
`?>`

Save the document in your web server's **/htdocs** directory as **search.php** then open the page via HTTP to see the search results

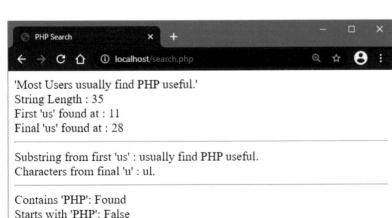

Hot tip

The **str_contains()**, **str_starts_with()** and **str_ends_with()** functions are great new features introduced in PHP 8.

95

Don't forget

There are two occurrences of **'us'** in this string. The initial **'Us'** is not matched by the case-sensitive searches.

Extracting substrings

A substring can be extracted from a string by stating the string, and index position of a substring within the string, as arguments to the **substr()** function. Optionally, a third argument can specify the substring length. You may replace a substring using the **substr_replace()** function to specify string, substring, index position and length arguments. The total number of occurrences of a substring within a string can be found using the **substr_count()** function:

substring.php

 Begin a PHP script with statements to initialize a variable with a string value and count substrings
```
<?php
$str = 'SQL in easy steps features SQL queries' ;
echo "'$str'<br>'SQL' Count: ".substr_count( $str , 'SQL' ) ;
```

 Next, add statements to extract two substrings
```
echo '<hr>Index 27 : '.substr( $str , 27 ) ;
echo '<hr>Index 4 Length 13 : '.substr( $str , 4 , 13 ) ;
```

 Now, add a statement to initialize a variable with a string
```
$sub = 'PHP & MySQL' ;
```

 Finally, add statements to replace a substring with a new string value and to display the modified string
```
$str = substr_replace( $str, $sub , 0 , 3 ) ;
echo "<hr>'$str'" ;
?>
```

Don't forget

The length argument in **substr_replace()** specifies the length of the substring to be replaced. In this example, it is **3** – to replace the three characters **'SQL'** with a longer string.

5 Save the document in your web browser's **/htdocs** directory as **substring.php** then open the page via HTTP to see the extracted substrings and modified string

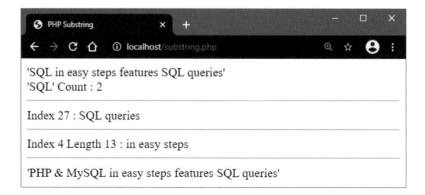

PHP Substring — localhost/substring.php

'SQL in easy steps features SQL queries'
'SQL' Count : 2

Index 27 : SQL queries

Index 4 Length 13 : in easy steps

'PHP & MySQL in easy steps features SQL queries'

Changing case

PHP provides functions to easily modify the character case of a specified string argument. The **strtolower()** function changes all characters to lowercase, and **strtoupper()** changes them all to uppercase. Additionally, the **ucfirst()** function makes only the first string character uppercase, whereas the **ucword()** function makes the first character of every word in the string uppercase:

1 Begin a PHP script with statements to initialize a variable with a string and display its value
```
<?php
$str = "C++ Programming in easy steps" ;
echo "Original String : '$str' <hr>" ;
```

case.php

2 Next, add statements to display a lowercase version
```
$ver = strtolower( $str ) ;
echo "Lowercase String : '$ver' <br>" ;
```

3 Now, add statements to display an uppercase version
```
$ver = strtoupper( $str ) ;
echo "Uppercase String : '$ver' <hr>" ;
```

Beware

4 Finally, add statements to display a capitalized string version and a capitalized words version
```
$ver = ucfirst( strtolower( $str ) ) ;
echo "Uppercase First String Character : '$ver' <br>" ;
echo 'Uppercase First Word Character : '.ucwords( $ver ) ;
?>
```

The **ucfirst()** function only changes the first character of a string. Other uppercase characters will remain unless first changed to lowercase with the **strtolower()** function, as seen here.

 Save the document in your web server's **/htdocs** directory as **case.php** then open the page via HTTP to see the changed case versions of the original string

```
PHP Case

→ C ⌂ ⓘ localhost/case.php

Original String : 'C++ Programming in easy steps'

Lowercase String : 'c++ programming in easy steps'
Uppercase String : 'C++ PROGRAMMING IN EASY STEPS'

Uppercase First String Character : 'C++ programming in easy steps'
Uppercase First Word Character : C++ Programming In Easy Steps
```

Formatting strings

PHP provides a number of built-in functions to conveniently format strings by manipulating their characters. The simple **strrev()** function accepts a single string argument and returns that string in reversed character order, so it reads back to front.

The **strrpt()** function accepts two arguments to specify a string, and an integer of how many total times that string should be repeated in the string it will return.

The **strpad()** function accepts three arguments to specify a string, a total length of the character string it will return, and a character or substring pattern with which to fill the difference between the original string and the specified returned string length. The padding will, by default, be added to the end of the original string but can be added to its start by adding a fourth argument using a special **STR_PAD_LEFT** flag.

The **trim()** function can accept a single string argument and will return a string in which all white-space characters (spaces, line returns, tabs) have been removed from the start and end of the original string. Optionally, a second argument can specify a character or pattern to be removed from the start and end of the original string, in place of the white-space default.

Similarly, where you only want to remove characters from the start of the original string, you can use the companion **ltrim()** function, or where you only want to remove characters from the end of the original string, you can use the companion **rtrim()** function.

A string can be split into individual parts using the **strtok()** function to specify the string and a delimiter token around which the parts should be split. For example, if you want to split a string into individual words, you can specify the space character as the delimiter token. The first part of the string, up to the delimiter token, will be returned by the function. Interestingly, the **strtok()** function remembers its position in the string, so subsequent calls need only specify the delimiter token to return the next part of the string, until no further delimiters are found. Splitting a string in this way can best be achieved using a loop to make subsequent calls to the **strtok()** function, until it reaches the end of the string.

The PHP **implode()** and **explode()** functions can be used to convert arrays to strings, and strings to arrays – see page 32 for more details.

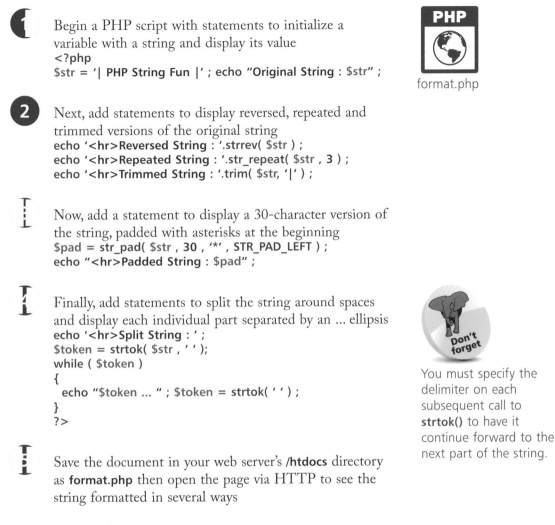

① Begin a PHP script with statements to initialize a variable with a string and display its value

```php
<?php
$str = '| PHP String Fun |' ; echo "Original String : $str" ;
```

format.php

② Next, add statements to display reversed, repeated and trimmed versions of the original string

```php
echo '<hr>Reversed String : '.strrev( $str ) ;
echo '<hr>Repeated String : '.str_repeat( $str , 3 ) ;
echo '<hr>Trimmed String : '.trim( $str, '|' ) ;
```

③ Now, add a statement to display a 30-character version of the string, padded with asterisks at the beginning

```php
$pad = str_pad( $str , 30 , '*' , STR_PAD_LEFT ) ;
echo "<hr>Padded String : $pad" ;
```

④ Finally, add statements to split the string around spaces and display each individual part separated by an ... ellipsis

```php
echo '<hr>Split String : ' ;
$token = strtok( $str , ' ' );
while ( $token )
{
  echo "$token ... " ; $token = strtok( ' ' ) ;
}
?>
```

You must specify the delimiter on each subsequent call to **strtok()** to have it continue forward to the next part of the string.

⑤ Save the document in your web server's **/htdocs** directory as **format.php** then open the page via HTTP to see the string formatted in several ways

Original String : | PHP String Fun |

Reversed String : | nuF gnirtS PHP |

Repeated String : | PHP String Fun || PHP String Fun || PHP String Fun |

Trimmed String : PHP String Fun

Padded String : ************| PHP String Fun |

Split String : | ... PHP ... String ... Fun ... | ...

Making dates

The PHP **date()** function will return a date string when called, but requires a string argument to specify a format for the date string. This format string can comprise a series of letter options for date and time. For example, **date('n/j/y')** might return "4/22/16". Popular options are listed below along with a brief description:

Option	Description	Example
Y	Year as four digits	2023
y	Year as two digits	14
n	Month as one or two digits	7
m	Month as two digits	07
F	Month full name	February
M	Month name as three letters	Feb
j	Day as one or two digits	4
d	Day as two digits	04
l	Weekday full name	Monday
D	Weekday as three letters	Mon
S	Ordinal suffix as two letters	th
H	Hour in 24-hour format	14
i	Minutes	45
s	Seconds	30
a	Ante or post meridiem	am

The weekday full name option is a lowercase "L".

Hot tip

You can discover more **date()** function options in the PHP manual online at **php.net/manual**

By default, the timezone is set to the Universal Time Clock (UTC) but you can set it to your own timezone by specifying it as an argument to the **date_default_timezone_set()** function, and see the currently-set timezone with **date_default_timezone_get()**.

You may also create your own timestamp using the intelligent **strtotime()** function. This can accept a date string argument and return a timestamp that can be supplied as an optional second argument to the **date()** function. The argument specified to **strtotime()** can be a regular text date, such as "July 4, 2023". Additionally, you can specify an argument such as "yesterday", "+3months" or "next Wednesday" and the **strtotime()** function will try to figure it out and return an appropriate timestamp.

...cont'd

Begin a PHP script with statements to display the current date, day, time and current default timezone

```php
<?php
echo 'Date : '.date( 'jS F Y' ).'<br>' ;
echo 'Day : '.date( 'l' ).'<br>' ;
echo 'Time : '.date( 'h:i:s a' ).'<br>' ;
echo 'Timezone : '.date_default_timezone_get().'<hr>' ;
```

date.php

Next, add statements to change the default timezone and display a confirmation, then show the current time there

```php
date_default_timezone_set( 'America/New_York' ) ;
echo 'Timezone now : '.date_default_timezone_get() ;
echo '<br>Time now : '.date( 'h:i:s a' ).'<hr>' ;
```

Now, add statements to create a timestamp for the next day, then display its day name and date

```php
$d = strtotime( 'tomorrow' ) ;
echo 'Tomorrow : '.date( 'l, jS F Y' , $d ).'<br>' ;
```

Hot tip

Notice that you can include separator characters such as : and / in the format string.

Finally, add statements to create a timestamp for a memorable date, then display its month and day number

```php
$d = strtotime( 'July 11, 1994' ) ;
echo 'David\'s Birthday : '.date( 'F jS' , $d ) ;
?>
```

Save the document in your web server's **/htdocs** directory as **date.php** then open the page via HTTP to see the date strings formatted by the options

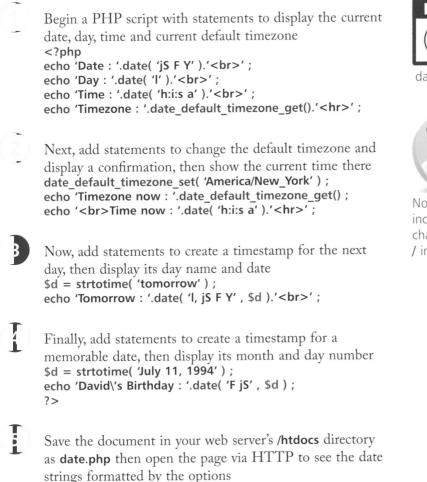

Don't forget

Some countries prefer date order of M/D/Y while others prefer D/M/Y so you can choose your preferred date format options.

Encoding entities

There are two PHP functions available to encode HTML code, so that all characters of special significance or unusual characters are replaced by "entity" equivalents. The **htmlentities()** function encodes all characters below, which each have an entity equivalent:

```
" & < >   ¡ ¢ £ ¤ ¥ ¦ § ¨ © ª « ¬ ® ¯ ° ± ² ³ ´ µ ¶ · ¸ ¹ º » ¼ ½ ¾ ¿ À Á Â Ã Ä
Å Æ Ç È É Ê Ë Ì Í Î Ï Ð Ñ Ò Ó Ô Õ Ö × Ø Ù Ú Û Ü Ý Þ ß à á â ã ä å æ ç è
é ê ë ì í î ï ð ñ ò ó ô õ ö ÷ ø ù ú û ü ý þ ÿ Œ œ Š š Ÿ ƒ ˆ ˜ Α Β Γ Δ Ε Ζ Η Θ Ι
Κ Λ Μ Ν Ξ Ο Π Ρ Σ Τ Υ Φ Χ Ψ Ω α β γ δ ε ζ η θ ι κ λ μ ν ξ ο π ρ ς σ τ υ φ
χ ψ ω ϑ ϒ ϖ   – — ' ' , " " „ † ‡ • … ‰ ′ ″ ‹ › ‾ ⁄ € ℑ ℘ ℜ ™ ℵ ← ↑
→ ↓ ↔ ↵ ⇐ ⇑ ⇒ ⇓ ⇔ ∀ ∂ ∃ ∅ ∇ ∈ ∉ ∋ ∏ ∑ − ∗ √ ∝ ∞ ∠ ∧ ∨ ∩ ∪ ∫ ∴ ∼ ≅
≈ ≠ ≡ ≤ ≥ ⊂ ⊃ ⊄ ⊆ ⊇ ⊕ ⊗ ⊥ ⋅ ⌈ ⌉ ⌊ ⌋ 〈 〉 ◊ ♠ ♣ ♥ ♦
```

102

Unless you are concerned about non-English language characters, it is generally preferable to use the alternative **htmlspecialchars()** function to encode only characters of special HTML significance:

● & ampersand – becomes **&**

● " double quote – becomes **"**

● ' single quote – becomes **'**

● < less than – becomes **<**

● > greater than – becomes **>**

One good reason to encode HTML snippets with PHP is to prevent malicious JavaScript code being executed unintentionally by the web browser. Encoding HTML tags into entities ensures that the HTML **<script>** tag will not be recognized, so its JavaScript code contents will not be executed:

encode.php

1 Create a PHP script with statements to initialize a variable with an HTML snippet and display its value
```php
<?php
$html = '<script>window.location="index.html"</script>' ;
// Statement to be inserted here.
echo $html ;
?>
```

2 Save the document in your web server's **/htdocs** directory as **encode.php** then open the page via HTTP to hopefully see the HTML code snippet

...cont'd

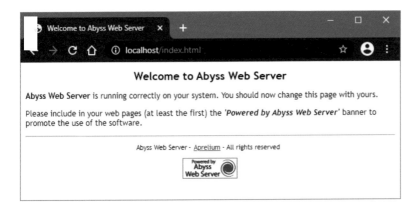

The browser has interpreted the code and relocated to the server's index page because it recognized the HTML **<script>** tag.

Return to the PHP script and insert a statement to encode special HTML characters
$html = htmlspecialchars($html) ;

4 Save the edited document and reopen the page via HTTP again to see the HTML code snippet

Use the **View Source** facility in your web browser to see the special character entity equivalents encoded by PHP

The PHP function **html_entity_decode()** can be used to unencode all entities back to their original character state.

103

Summary

- The PHP built-in string comparison functions **strcmp()**, **strncmp()**, **strcasecmp()** and **strncasecmp()** each typically return a result of 1 (greater), 0 (equal) or -1 (less).

- String comparisons are based on the numerical ASCII value of each character, compared in sequence to account for order.

- The ASCII value of any character can be found using **ord()**.

- The length of any string can be found using **strlen()**.

- The numerical index position of a substring within a searched string can be found using **strpos()** and **strrpos()** functions.

- The search functions **strstr()**, **stristr()**, **strchr()** and **strrchr()** each return the remainder of a searched string on success.

- The substring functions **substr()**, **substr_replace()** and **substr_count()** can extract, replace or count occurrences.

- The characters in a string can be reversed using **strrev()**, or the string can be repeated using **strrpt()**.

- Padding characters can be added to a string using **strpad()** and characters can be removed using **trim()**, **ltrim()** or **rtrim()**.

- A string can be split into individual parts by specifying a delimiter to the **strtok()** function.

- The **date()** function requires a string argument that specifies options to determine the format of its returned date string.

- By default, the PHP date timezone is set to UTC.

- The **date_default_timezone_set()** function can be used to specify an alternative to the UTC default timezone.

- The **strtotime()** function will attempt to return an appropriate timestamp for whatever date or time argument it receives.

- The **htmlentities()** function will encode all string characters for which there is an equivalent entity.

- The **htmlspecialchars()** function will encode only characters of special HTML significance to avoid recognition by a browser.

7 Building classes

This chapter demonstrates   **106** **Encapsulating data**

how to create and use   **108** **Creating an object**

virtual objects for Object   **110** **Initializing members**

Oriented Programming   **112** **Using constructors**

with PHP.   **114** **Promoting properties**

                               116 **Inheriting properties**

                               118 **Embracing polymorphism**

                               120 **Chaining method calls**

                               122 **Summary**

Encapsulating data

A class is a data structure that can contain both variables and functions in a single entity. These are collectively known as its "members" – the variables are known as its class "properties" and the functions are known as its class "methods".

Access to class members from outside the class is controlled by "access specifiers" in the class declaration. Typically, these will deny access to the class variables but allow access to methods that can store and retrieve data from those variable members. This technique of "data hiding" ensures that stored data is safely encapsulated within the class variable members, and is the first principle of Object Oriented Programming (OOP).

A class declaration begins with the **class** keyword, followed by a space, then a programmer-specified name – adhering to the usual PHP naming conventions but beginning in uppercase. Next come the class property declarations followed by the class method declarations. These are like regular variable and function declarations but should each begin with an access specifier. The class declaration syntax looks like this:

```
class ClassName
{
  access-specifier $var1 , $var2 , $var3 ;

  access-specifier functionName1 ( $arg1 , $arg2 , $arg3 )
  {
    statements-to-execute ;
  }
}
```

Hot tip

It is conventional to begin class names with an uppercase character and object names with lowercase.

An access specifier may be any one of the keywords **public**, **private** or **protected**, to specify access rights for its listed members:

● **public** members are accessible from any place where the class is visible.

● **private** members are accessible only to other members of the same class in which they are defined.

● **protected** members are accessible only to other members of the same class and members of classes derived from that class.

Hot tip

Derived classes are introduced later in this chapter – see page 116.

Any real-world object can be defined by its attributes and by its actions. For example, a dog has attributes such as age, weight and color, and actions it can perform such as bark. The class mechanism in PHP provides a way to create a virtual dog object within a script, where the class properties can represent its attributes and the class methods represent its actions:

```php
class Dog
{
  private $age ;
  private $weight ;
  private $color ;

  public function bark() { echo 'WOOF!' ; }

  // Plus methods here to store data in the properties.

  // Plus methods here to retrieve data from the properties.

}
```

Don't forget

While a PHP script class cannot perfectly emulate a real-word object, the aim is to encapsulate all relevant attributes and actions as class properties and methods.

It is important to recognize that a class declaration only defines a data structure – in order to create an object you must declare an "instance" of that data structure. This is achieved by assigning a copy of a class to a variable using the **new** keyword, like this:

```php
$fido = new Dog() ;      // Creates an instance named "fido"
                         // of the programmer-defined
                         // "Dog" data structure.
```

The instance object is a working copy of the original class data structure so retains all its features. As the method in the example above has been declared **public**, it is visible in the script outside the class declaration. This means the instance's copy of the method can be called using a special -> object operator, like this:

```php
$fido->bark() ;          // Outputs WOOF!
```

The -> object operator can be used to reference any visible class member, but the variable properties in the example above have been declared **private** so are encapsulated in the object and are not directly accessible. The principle of encapsulation in PHP programming describes the grouping together of data and functionality in class members – these are the age, weight, color attributes and bark action in this Dog class.

Beware

Notice that you must add parentheses after the class name in the statement creating an instance object.

107

Creating an object

In order to assign and retrieve data from private members of a class, special **public** accessor methods must be added to the class. These are "setter" methods to assign data, and "getter" methods to retrieve data. Accessor methods are often named as the variable they address, with the first letter made uppercase, and prefixed by "set" or "get" respectively. For example, accessor methods to address an **age** variable may be named **setAge()** and **getAge()**.

The setter and getter methods can reference a member of the same class using a special **$this** "pseudo-variable", followed by the **->** object operator, and the property name. For example, using **$this->age** to reference an age property:

object.php

 1 Begin a PHP script with a statement to declare a class named "Dog"
```php
<?php
class Dog
{
   // Members to be inserted here (Steps 2-5).
}
```

2 Between the braces of the Dog class declaration, declare three private variable members
```php
private $age ;
private $weight ;
private $color ;
```

3 After the private variables, add a public method to output a string when called
```php
public function bark() { echo 'WOOF! WOOF! <br>' ; }
```

4 Add public setter methods – to assign individual argument values to each of the private variables
```php
public function setAge ( int $yrs )
{ $this->age = $yrs ; }

public function setWeight ( int $lbs )
{ $this->weight = $lbs ; }

public function setColor ( string $fur )
{ $this->color = $fur ; }
```

Hot tip

In the class declaration, notice that all methods are declared public and all variables are declared private. This notion of "public interface, private data" is a key concept when creating classes.

Add public getter methods – to retrieve individual values
from each of the private variables
public function getAge() { return $this->age ; }

public function getWeight() { return $this->weight ; }

public function getColor() { return $this->color ; }

Fido

After the Dog class declaration, declare an instance of the
Dog class named "fido"
$fido = new Dog() ;

Add statements calling each setter method to assign data
$fido->setAge(3) ;
$fido->setWeight(15) ;
$fido->setColor('brown') ;

Add statements calling each getter method to retrieve the
assigned values
**echo 'Fido is a '.$fido->getColor().' dog
' ;**
**echo 'Fido is '.$fido->getAge().' years old
' ;**
**echo 'Fido weighs '.$fido->getWeight().' pounds
' ;**

Now, add a call to the regular output method
$fido->bark() ;
?>

Save the document in your web server's **/htdocs** directory
as **object.php** then open the page via HTTP to see the
output class properties and method call

Hot tip

This **object.php** script
will get modified over
the next few pages
as new features are
incorporated.

Initializing members

A program can easily create multiple objects simply by declaring multiple instances of a class, and each object can have unique attributes by assigning individual values with its setter methods.

It is often convenient to combine the setter methods into a single method that accepts arguments for each private variable. This means that all values can be assigned with a single statement in the program, but the method will contain multiple statements.

Optionally, each parameter can specify a permissible data type for each argument being passed, and may also usefully specify default values to each parameter:

initializer.php

1 Rename a copy of the previous example "object.php" as a new program "initializer.php"

2 In the Dog class declaration, replace the three setter methods with a single combined setter method that specifies the argument data types and default values
```
public function setValues
( int $yrs = 2 , int $lbs = 8 , string $fur = 'black' )
{
   // Statements to be inserted here.
}
```

3 In the method definition block, insert three statements to assign values from passed arguments to class variables
```
$this->age = $yrs ;
$this->weight = $lbs ;
$this->color = $fur ;
```

4 After the modified class definition, replace the calls to the three setter methods by a single call to the combined setter method – passing three arguments
```
$fido->setValues( 3 , 15 , 'brown' ) ;
```

5 Declare a second instance of the Dog class named "pooch"
```
$pooch = new Dog() ;
```

6 Add a second call to the combined setter method – passing three arguments for the new object
```
$pooch->setValues( 4, 18, 'gray' ) ;
```

Hot tip

Try passing an incorrect data type to the initializer method to see a type error occur.

...cont'd

 Add statements calling each getter method to retrieve the assigned values
```
echo '<hr>Pooch: '.$pooch->getAge().'yrs' ;
echo $pooch->getWeight().'lbs '.$pooch->getColor() ;
```

8 Add a second call to the regular output method
```
$pooch->bark() ;
```

9 Now, declare a third instance of the Dog class named "rover"
```
$rover = new Dog() ;
```

10 Add a third call to the combined setter method – this time passing no arguments for the new object
```
$rover->setValues( ) ;
```

 Add statements calling each getter method to retrieve the assigned values, which are specified default values
```
echo '<hr>Rover: '.$rover->getAge().'yrs' ;
echo $rover->getWeight().'lbs '.$rover->getColor() ;
```

12 Add a third call to the regular output method
```
$rover->bark() ;
```

13 Save the document in your web server's **/htdocs** directory as **initializer.php** then open the page via HTTP to see the output set by the combined initializer method

You must still call the initializer method here, to assign the default values to the class variables when passing no arguments.

Using constructors

Class variable members can be initialized by a special "constructor" method that is called whenever an instance of the class is created. The constructor method is always named **__construct()** and can accept arguments to set the initial value of class variables.

A constructor method has a companion "destructor" method – that is called whenever an instance of the class is destroyed. The destructor method is always named **__destruct()**.

Constructor and destructor methods have no return value and are called automatically – they cannot be called explicitly, and consequently their declarations need no access specifier.

Values to initialize class variables are passed to the constructor method in the statement creating an object, in parentheses following the object name:

constructor.php

1 Rename a copy of the previous example "initializer.php" as a new program "constructor.php"

2 In the Dog class declaration, replace the setValues method with this constructor
```
function __construct
( int $yrs = 2 , int $lbs = 8 , string $fur = 'black' )
{
  $this->age = $yrs ;
  $this->weight = $lbs ;
  $this->color = $fur ;
}
```

3 Now, add a simple destructor method
```
function __destruct() { echo '<hr>Object Destroyed.' ; }
```

Hot tip

The definition of a class method is also known as the method "implementation".

4 After the Dog class declaration, edit the statement creating the "fido" object – to pass values to its constructor method, in order to initialize properties
```
$fido = new Dog( 3 , 15 , 'brown' ) ;
```

5 Similarly, edit the statement creating the "pooch" object – to pass values to the constructor method
```
$pooch = new Dog( 4 , 18 , 'gray' ) ;
```

...cont'd

Also edit the statement creating the "rover" object – to use default values of the constructor method
$rover = new Dog( ) ;

7   Delete the statements calling the setValues method of all three objects – the constructor now replaces that method

PHP provides several functions to interrogate classes such as **class_exists(*class*)**, **method_exists(*class*, *method*)**, and **property_exists(*class*, *property*)** that return **TRUE** on success. You can also get a list of class members with **get_class_vars(*class*)** and **get_class_methods(*class*)** to see only "visible" members:

8   Add statements to display the total number of accessible variables in the Dog class
$items = get_class_vars('Dog') ;
**echo '
Dog variables : '.count($items) ;**

Add statements to display the names of accessible methods in the Dog class
**echo '
Dog methods :' ;**
$items = get_class_methods('Dog') ;
foreach($items as $item) { echo "$item, " ; }

10   Save the document in your web server's **/htdocs** directory as **constructor.php** then open the page via HTTP to see the output set by the constructor

Although the initial values of the variable members are set by the constructor, setter methods can be added to subsequently change the values – and those new values can be retrieved by the getter methods.

The number of visible variables is zero. Temporarily change their access specifier to public and see it become 3 – encapsulation in action.

Promoting properties

The typical syntax to create a class that declares a property then assigns a value to it in the constructor is quite verbose:

```
class ClassName
{
  access-specifier type $property ;

  function __construct( type $arg )
  {
    $this->property = $arg ;
  }
}
```

Happily, this can be simplified by adding one of the access specifiers (**public, private** or **protected**) before parameters of the constructor method. This "promotes" the parameters so that properties of the parameter names will be automatically added to the class, along with a forwarding assignment to those properties in the body of the constructor method. Constructor property promotion is shorthand syntax to declare and assign class properties from the constructor. There is no need to declare the property first, so the syntax now looks like this:

```
class ClassName
{
  function __construct ( access-specifier type $property ) {  }
}
```

The body of the constructor can still contain statements to execute and properties can be accessed using setter and getter methods of the class as usual.

Hot tip

The ability to promote class properties in the constructor is a great new feature introduced in PHP 8.

promoter.php

1 Begin a PHP script with a statement to declare a class using standard properties

```php
<?php
class Paint_1
{
  private string $color ;

  function __construct( string $hue = 'Blue' )
  {
    $this->color = $hue ;
  }

  public function setColor( string $c ){ $this->color = $c ; }
  public function getColor(){ return $this->color ; }
}
```

2   Next, in the script, add a statement to create an instance of the class
```php
$pot_1 = new Paint_1() ;
```

3   Now, add statements to call the class methods
```php
echo $pot_1->getColor().'<br>' ;
echo $pot_1->setColor( 'Yellow' ) ;
echo $pot_1->getColor().'<hr>' ;
```

Don't forget

Only the __construct() method can have promoted properties.

4   Then, declare a similar class with simplified syntax using promoted properties
```php
class Paint_2
{
  function __construct( private string $color = 'Red' ) { }
  public function setColor( string $c ){ $this->color = $c ; }
  public function getColor(){ return $this->color ; }
}
```

5   Next, in the script, add a statement to create an instance of the similar class
```php
$pot_2 = new Paint_2() ;
```

6   Finally, add statements to call the similar class methods
```php
echo $pot_2->getColor().'<br>' ;
echo $pot_2->setColor( 'Green' ) ;
echo $pot_2->getColor() ;
?>
```

Hot tip

It is technically possible to mix standard properties and promoted properties but this can produce unclear code – use only one technique.

7   Save the document in your web server's **/htdocs** directory as **promoter.php** then open the page via HTTP to see the output from the standard and promoted properties

Inheriting properties

A PHP class can be created as a brand new class, like those in previous examples, or can be "derived" from an existing class. Importantly, a derived class inherits members of the parent (base) class from which it is derived – in addition to its own members.

The ability to inherit members from a base class allows derived classes to be created that share certain common properties, which have been defined in the base class. For example, a "Polygon" base class may define width and height properties that are common to all polygons. Classes of "Rectangle" and Triangle" could be derived from the Polygon class – inheriting width and height properties, in addition to their own members defining their unique features.

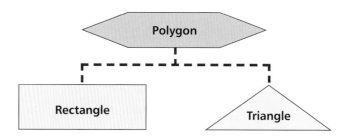

The virtue of inheritance is extremely powerful and is the second principle of Object Oriented Programming (OOP).

A derived class declaration adds the **extends** keyword after its class name, followed by the name of the class from which it derives:

inheritance.php

1 Begin a PHP script by declaring a base class named "Polygon", which has two private variables initialized by the constructor, and has two public getter methods

```php
<?php
class Polygon
{
  private $width , $height ;

  function __construct( int $w = 4 , int $h = 5 )
  {
    $this->width = $w ;
    $this->height = $h ;
  }

  public function getWidth() { return $this->width ; }
  public function getHeight() { return $this->height ; }
}
```

2 After the Polygon class, declare a "Rectangle" class that derives from the Polygon class and adds a unique method

```
class Rectangle extends Polygon
{
  public function area()
  {
    return ( $this->getWidth() * $this->getHeight() ) ;
  }
}
```

3 After the Rectangle class, declare a "Triangle" class that derives from the Polygon class and adds a unique method

```
class Triangle extends Polygon
{
  public function area()
  {
    return ( $this->getWidth() * $this->getHeight() / 2 ) ;
  }
}
```

4 After the Triangle class, add two statements creating an instance of each derived class using default values

```
$rect = new Rectangle() ;
$trio = new Triangle() ;
```

5 Finally, add two statements to output the value returned by the unique method of each derived class

```
echo 'Rectangle Area : '.$rect->area().'<hr>' ;
echo 'Triangle Area : '.$trio->area() ;
?>
```

6 Save the document in your web server's **/htdocs** directory as **inheritance.php** then open the page via HTTP to see the output from inherited members

Don't confuse class instances and derived classes – an instance is a copy of a class, whereas a derived class is a new class that inherits properties of the base class from which it is derived.

In PHP, a derived class is always dependent on a single base class – multiple inheritance is not supported.

117

Embracing polymorphism

The three cornerstones of Object Oriented Programming (OOP) are encapsulation, inheritance, and polymorphism. On the previous pages we have seen how data can be encapsulated within a PHP class, and how derived classes inherit the properties of their base class, so we can now explore the final cornerstone principle of polymorphism.

The term "polymorphism" (from Greek, meaning "many forms") describes the ability to assign a different meaning or purpose to an entity according to its context. For example, in the real world everyone knows how to use a push button (entity) – you simply apply pressure to it. What that button does, however, depends on what is connected to it (context), but the result does not affect how that button is used.

In the world of Object Oriented Programming, polymorphism allows classes to have different functionality while sharing a common interface. The interface does not need to know which class it is using because they are, like the real world button, all used the same way, but can produce different contextual results. Embracing polymorphism in this way enables the programmer to create interchangeable objects that can be selected according to requirement, rather than by conditional tests.

A PHP interface is similar to a class but is declared using the **interface** keyword and can only contain method definitions, not any method statements to be executed, like this:

interface *InterfaceName*
{
   // Method definitions only go here.
}

Don't forget

Method definitions in a interface declaration may also specify parameters.

Each class that implements an interface must implement all the methods it defines by specifying their statements to be executed. A class is attached to an interface by including the **implements** keyword and interface name in its declaration, like this:

class *ClassName* implements *InterfaceName*
{
   // Method implementations go here.
}

The previous example can be modified to embrace polymorphism by adding an interface and a single function.

polymorphism.php

l) Rename a copy of the previous example "inheritance.php" as a new program "polymorphism.php"

2) Declare an interface named "Shape", which contains a definition for the methods already implemented in the Rectangle and Triangle classes
interface Shape { public function area() ; }

3) Edit the first line of the Rectangle and Triangle class declarations – to associate them with the interface
class Rectangle extends Polygon implements Shape
class Triangle extends Polygon implements Shape

4) After the class blocks, add a function that accepts an argument of the Shape type and calls its defined method
function getArea(Shape $shape)
{ return $shape->area() ; }

Hot tip

5) Edit the two statements creating an instance of each derived class – to pass in argument values
$rect = new Rectangle(8 , 10) ;
$trio = new Triangle(8 , 10) ;

6) Finally, edit the two statements to output the value returned by the unique method of each derived class, by calling each method via the interface
echo 'Rectangle Area : '.getArea($rect).'<hr>' ;
echo 'Triangle Area : '.getArea($trio) ;

7) Save the document in your web server's **/htdocs** directory as **polymorphism.php** then open the page via HTTP to see the output via a polymorphic interface

What's going on here?

Each call to the new **getArea()** function passes an instance object as an argument.

The **getArea()** function calls the **area()** method defined in the interface.

The output is returned from the implementation of the **area()** method of the associated instance.

119

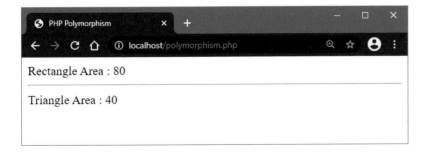

PHP Polymorphism

localhost/polymorphism.php

Rectangle Area : 80

Triangle Area : 40

Chaining method calls

You may often want to call a method, or get a property, only if the result of one or more tested expressions are not **null**. This can quickly lead to deeply nested conditional tests, like these:

```
$country = null ;

if( $session !== null )
{
   $user = $session->user ;
   if ( $user !== null )
   {
      $address = $user->getAddress() ;
      if( $address !== null )
      {
         $country = $address->country ;
      }
   }
}
```

The **?->** nullsafe operator is a great new feature introduced in PHP 8.

The same series of conditional tests can be made more concisely in a single chain using the PHP **?->** "nullsafe" operator, like this:

```
$country = $session?->user?->getAddress()?->country ;
```

The chain is evaluated from left to right. When the item at the left of the nullsafe operator evaluates to **null**, the execution of the entire chain stops immediately and the chain evaluates to **null**.

nullsafe.php

 Begin a PHP script by declaring a class that assigns a **null** value to a property
```
class Session
{
  public $user ;
  function __construct() { $this->user = null ; }
}
```

 Declare a class containing a method to return an object
```
class User
{
  public function getAddress() { return new Address() ; }
}
```

Declare a class that assigns a **string** value to a property
```
class Address
{
  public $country ;
  function __construct() { $this->country = 'USA' ; }
}
```

4 Then, create an instance of the class declared in Step 1
$session = new Session() ;

Finally, add a chain statement without nullsafe operators
that attempts to output the **string** property
$country = $session->user->getAddress()->country ;
echo 'Location: '.$country ;

6 Save the document in your web server's **/htdocs** directory
as **nullsafe.php** then open the page via HTTP to see the
attempt fail with a fatal error message

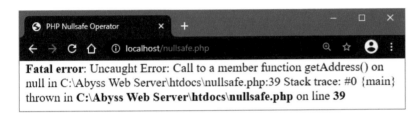

Fatal error: Uncaught Error: Call to a member function getAddress() on
null in C:\Abyss Web Server\htdocs\nullsafe.php:39 Stack trace: #0 {main}
thrown in **C:\Abyss Web Server\htdocs\nullsafe.php** on line **39**

Edit the chain statement in Step 5 to add nullsafe
operators, then save the script and refresh the browser to
see the attempt fail gracefully
$country = $session?->user?->getAddress()?->country ;

Hot tip

Skipping evaluation of
the remainder of the
chain when an item
in a chain evaluates to
null is known as "short
circuiting". When the
item at the left hand side
of the nullsafe operator
does not evaluate to
null, execution continues
to evaluate the next item
in the chain until the end
of the chain is reached.

Location:

8 Edit the assignment in Step 1 to assign an object to the
property, then save the script once more and refresh the
browser to see the attempt succeed
function __construct() { $this->user = new User() ; }

Location: USA

Summary

- A PHP class is a data structure that can contain both variables and functions in a single entity.

- Classes are declared using the **class** keyword and can contain member variable properties and member function methods.

- Access to class members from outside the class is controlled by the **public, private** or **protected** access specifier keywords.

- Variable properties are encapsulated by declaring them **private** so their values can only be accessed by **public** methods.

- In order to create an object you must declare an instance of a **class** data structure using the **new** keyword.

- The special -> object operator can be used to reference any visible class member.

- Setter and getter methods can reference a member of the same class using the **$this** pseudo-variable.

- The **__construct()** constructor method is called when a class is created and can be used to initialize variable properties.

- Adding **public, private** or **protected** access specifiers for constructor parameters can promote properties to the class.

- The **__destruct()** destructor method is called when a class is destroyed and can be used to execute final statements.

- PHP has functions to interrogate classes, listing methods with **get_class_methods()** and variables with **get_class_vars()**.

- The three cornerstones of Object Oriented Programming are encapsulation, inheritance, and polymorphism.

- A derived class declaration will include the **extends** keyword to specify a base class from which to inherit members.

- An interface is declared using the **interface** keyword and the declaration may contain only method definitions.

- A class is attached to an interface by including the **implements** keyword and interface name in its declaration.

- Conditional tests for null values can be made concisely in a single chain using the PHP **?->** "nullsafe" operator.

8 Handling files

This chapter demonstrates **124** **Reading files**

how to read and write files **126** **Reading lines**

with PHP and how to deal **127** **Reading characters**

with errors in scripts. **128** **Writing a file**

130 **Appending text**

132 **Handling errors**

134 **Catching exceptions**

136 **Summary**

Reading files

The ability to read and write files located on the web server is useful to log information and to provide page content. In order to process files, a "filestream" object must first be created using the PHP **fopen()** function. This requires two arguments to specify the name or path of the file and a file "mode". The file mode determines the nature of the operation to be performed and places the file pointer at a suitable position within the file:

The file mode specifier must appear within quote marks when supplied as an argument to the **fopen()** function.

File mode	Operation
r	Open an existing file to read File pointer starts at the beginning of the file
w	Discard all contents of an existing file or create a new file if none exists File pointer starts at the beginning of the file
a	Open an existing file and preserve all contents File pointer starts at the end of the file
r+	Open a file to read from or write to File pointer starts at the beginning of the file
w+	Open a file to write to or read from Discard all contents of an existing file or create a new file if none exists File pointer starts at the beginning of the file
a+	Open a file to read from or write to and preserve all contents File pointer starts at the end of the file

Specify an explanatory message as an argument to the **die()** function.

It is good practice to always provide an alternative with the **die()** function in case the attempt to create a filestream fails.

When a filestream is created successfully, the file can be read by specifying the filestream and byte size as arguments to the **fread()** function. If the whole file is to be read it is convenient to use the **filesize()** function to specify the byte size of the file to be read.

Upon completion of any file operation, the filestream must be destroyed by specifying it as an argument to the **fclose()** function.

...cont'd

manifesto.txt

1. Begin a PHP script with statements that attempt to open a plain text file for reading, or exit the script upon failure
```
<?php
$filestream = fopen( 'manifesto.txt' , 'r' )
or die( 'Unable to open file!' ) ;
```

read.php

2. Next, add a statement to read the text file upon success and display its entire contents
```
echo fread( $filestream , filesize( 'manifesto.txt' ) ) ;
```

3. Now, remember to close the filestream
```
fclose( $filestream ) ;
```

4. Save the document in your web server's **/htdocs** directory as **read.php**, alongside the plain text file to be read, then open the page via HTTP to see the text file contents displayed in the browser window

Unlike a PHP block within an HTML document, a purely PHP script needs no closing **?>** tag.

125

Notice that the output here does not maintain line endings – but the example on page 126 does.

Reading lines

Once a "filestream" object is created, its contents can be read one line at a time by specifying the filestream as an argument to the PHP **fgets()** function. To read every line, this function can be called repeatedly in a loop. The **feof()** function can determine when the end of the file is reached and can end the loop:

The **feof()** function returns true when the end of the file is reached.

```
manifesto.txt - Notepad                                    —    □    ×
File  Edit  Format  View  Help
The workers have nothing to lose in this [revolution] but
their chains.
They have a world to gain.
Workers of the world unite!

- Karl Marx , The Communist Manifesto 1848
```

readlines.php

 1 Begin a PHP script with statements that attempt to open a plain text file for reading, or exit the script upon failure
```
<?php
$filestream = fopen( 'manifesto.txt' , 'r' )
or die( 'Unable to open file!' ) ;
```

 2 Next, add a loop to read the text file line-by-line upon success and display its entire contents
```
while( !feof( $filestream ) )
{ echo fgets( $filestream ).'<br>' ; }
```

3 Now, remember to close the filestream
```
fclose( $filestream ) ;
```

The next to last line is not actually empty – it contains an invisible newline character.

4 Save the document in your web server's **/htdocs** directory as **readlines.php**, alongside the plain text file to be read, then open the page via HTTP to see the text file lines

```
localhost/readlines.php    ×    +                          —    □    ×
←  →  C  ⌂  ⓘ localhost/readlines.php              ⊕  ☆  ⊖  :

The workers have nothing to lose in this [revolution] but their chains.
They have a world to gain.
Workers of the world unite!

- Karl Marx , The Communist Manifesto 1848
```

Reading characters

Once a "filestream" object is created, its contents can be read one character at a time by specifying the filestream as an argument to the PHP **fgetc()** function. To read every character, this function can be called repeatedly in a loop. The **fgetc()** function will return false when the end of the file is reached and can end the loop:

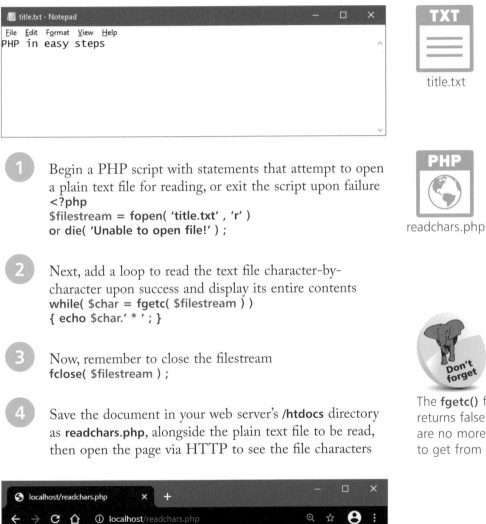

1. Begin a PHP script with statements that attempt to open a plain text file for reading, or exit the script upon failure
```php
<?php
$filestream = fopen( 'title.txt' , 'r' )
or die( 'Unable to open file!' ) ;
```

title.txt

readchars.php

2. Next, add a loop to read the text file character-by-character upon success and display its entire contents
```php
while( $char = fgetc( $filestream ) )
{ echo $char.' * ' ; }
```

3. Now, remember to close the filestream
```php
fclose( $filestream ) ;
```

4. Save the document in your web server's **/htdocs** directory as **readchars.php**, alongside the plain text file to be read, then open the page via HTTP to see the file characters

The **fgetc()** function returns false when there are no more characters to get from the stream.

Writing a file

Once a "filestream" object has been created specifying a write mode, a text file can be created. Text can be written into the file by specifying the filestream and a file name to the PHP **fwrite()** function. To format the text, non-printing invisible characters can also be written to create line breaks and tab spacing:

Character	Description
\n	Newline Move to a new line down
\r	Carriage return Move to the beginning of the line
\t	Tab Move along the line to the next tab stop

write.php

1. Begin a PHP script with a statement to assign text, including non-printing characters for formatting

```php
<?php
$poem = "\r\n\tI never saw a man who looked" ;
$poem .= "\r\n\tWith such a wistful eye" ;
$poem .= "\r\n\tUpon that little tent of blue" ;
$poem .= "\r\n\tWhich prisoners call the sky" ;
```

2. Next, assign a name for the file to be written

```php
$filename = 'poem.txt' ;
```

3. Attempt to create a plain text file for writing, or exit the script upon failure

```php
$filestream = fopen( $filename , 'w' )
or die( 'Unable to open file!' ) ;
```

4. Write the file and display a confirmation of how many bytes have been written in total

```php
$num = fwrite( $filestream , $poem ) ;
if( $num )
{
  echo "$num bytes written to $filename" ;
}
```

5. Now, remember to close the filestream

```php
fclose( $filestream ) ;
```

Beware

Strings containing non-printing characters must be enclosed within double quotes so that PHP can interpret them.

6 Save the document in your web server's **/htdocs** directory as **write.php** then open the page via HTTP to see confirmation that the text file has been written

120 bytes written to poem.txt

The folder where a file is to be written must have write permission.

7 Use File Explorer to navigate to your web server's **/htdocs** directory and see the file created by the PHP script

8 Open the file to see the text written by the PHP script

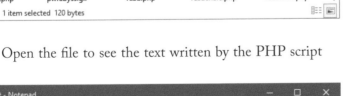

```
I never saw a man who looked
With such a wistful eye
Upon that little tent of blue
Which prisoners call the sky
```

You can run this example repeatedly and each time it will erase the content then write it again.

129

Appending text

Once a "filestream" object has been created specifying an append mode, a text file can be opened to add text at its end. Text can be appended to the file by specifying the filestream and a file name to the PHP **fwrite()** function. The process is identical to writing a file, except that the file pointer is positioned at the end of existing content before the text is written into the file:

append.php

1. Begin a PHP script with a statement to assign text, including non-printing characters for formatting
```
<?php
$info = "\r\n\r\n\tThe Ballad of Reading Gaol" ;
$info .= "\r\n\t\t\tOscar Wilde 1898" ;
```

2. Next, assign a name for the file to be written into
```
$filename = 'poem.txt' ;
```

3. Attempt to open the plain text file for appending, or exit the script upon failure
```
$filestream = fopen( $filename , 'a' )
or die( 'Unable to open file!' ) ;
```

4. Write the text and display a confirmation of how many bytes have been appended in total
```
$num = fwrite( $filestream , $info ) ;
if( $num )
{
  echo "$num bytes appended to $filename" ;
}
```

5. Now, remember to close the filestream
```
fclose( $filestream ) ;
```

6. Save the document in your web server's **/htdocs** directory as **append.php** then open the page via HTTP to see confirmation that the text has been appended to the file

Don't forget

Remember that non-printing characters must be enclosed in double quotes for interpretation.

130

52 bytes appended to poem.txt

...cont'd

7 Navigate to your web server's **/htdocs** directory and open the file to see the text appended by the PHP script

```
poem.txt - Notepad                                    —  □  ×
File  Edit  Format  View  Help
      I never saw a man who looked
      With such a wistful eye
      Upon that little tent of blue
      Which prisoners call the sky

      The Ballad of Reading Gaol
                    Oscar Wilde 1898
```

Overwriting text

It is important to recognize that when you write to an existing file in write mode it will overwrite any existing content:

1 Begin a PHP script by attempting to open an existing text file for writing, or exit the script upon failure
```php
<?php
$filestream = fopen( 'poem.txt' , 'w' )
or die( 'Unable to open file!' ) ;
```

overwrite.php

2 Upon success, write new text into the file
```php
fwrite( $filestream , 'Overwritten!' ) ;
```

3 Now, remember to close the filestream
```php
fclose( $filestream ) ;
```

4 Save the document in your web server's **/htdocs** directory as **overwrite.php** then open the page via HTTP and reopen the text file to see its contents overwritten

Be careful when writing to files as it is easy to accidentally overwrite.

```
poem.txt - Notepad                                    —  □  ×
File  Edit  Format  View  Help
Overwritten!
```

131

Handling errors

You can anticipate possible errors and terminate a running script when they occur using the **die()** function or the **exit()** function. Without this contingency, the default PHP error handler provides a useful but unsightly message when an error occurs. For example, **fopen('nonsuch.txt' , 'r')** to open a non-existing file:

Warning: fopen(nonsuch.txt): Failed to open stream: No such file or directory in **C:\Abyss Web Server\htdocs\nonsuch.php** on line **3**

Hot tip

The **die()** and **exit()** functions perform identical operations in PHP, but their terminology can have different appeals. For some, **die()** possibly seems more appropriate to quit when an error is detected, and **exit()** may seem more suitable to quit in other scenarios.

It is not always desirable to terminate a script when an error occurs, but you can create a custom error handler to provide a more user-friendly message than that provided by the default PHP error handler. A custom error handler is simply a function with this syntax:

function error_handler(*level* , *message* , *file* , *line* , *context*)

Only the first two parameters are required, the rest are optional. The first of these is a numerical value, representing a constant, indicating the severity of the error that has occurred:

Hot tip

The basic error levels are listed in this table but the PHP manual lists many more (**php.net/manual**).

Level	Constant	Description
2	E_WARNING	Non-fatal runtime error
8	E_NOTICE	Non-fatal possible error
256	E_USER_ERROR	Fatal user-generated error
512	E_USER_WARNING	Non-fatal user-generated error

A custom error handler function is nominated to handle errors by specifying its function name as the argument to the built-in PHP **set_error_handler()** function.

The error handler is called when an error occurs, or can be called explicitly using the **trigger_error()** function to specify an error message as its argument.

1 Begin a PHP script by defining a custom error handler function to report an error level and error message

```php
<?php
function error_handler( $level , $message )
{
  switch( $level )
  {
    case 2 : $str = 'Warning!' ;   break ;
    case 8 : $str = 'Notice!' ;    break ;
    default : $str = 'Error!' ;
  }
  echo "<b>$str</b><br>$message<hr>";
}
```

error.php

2 Next, nominate the function to handle errors

```php
set_error_handler( 'error_handler' ) ;
```

3 Now, for some mischief – attempt to access an uninitialized variable and try to open a non-existing file

```php
echo( $var ) ;
$file = fopen( 'nonsuch.txt' , 'r' ) ;
```

4 Explicitly trigger the custom error handler

```php
$number = 2 ;
if( $number >= 1 )
{
  trigger_error( 'Value of number must be 1 or less' ) ;
}
```

Don't forget

Notice that the script continues after reporting each error; it does not terminate on error.

5 Save the document in your web server's **/htdocs** directory as **error.php** then open the page via HTTP to see the error levels and appropriate messages

133

Catching exceptions

We can choose how a script should proceed when a specific error condition occurs. This error condition is called an "exception". When an exception occurs it is said to be "thrown", and code handling the exception is said to be its "catch". If an exception is not caught, PHP will treat it as a fatal error and issue an unsightly "Uncaught Exception" message – something like this:

Each **try** block must have an associated **catch** block, otherwise a fatal Uncaught Exception error will occur.

Fatal error: Uncaught Exception: Number : 5 Value must exceed 10 in C:\Abyss Web Server\htdocs\uncaught.php:8 Stack trace: #0 C:\Abyss Web Server\htdocs\uncaught.php(11): check_size() #1 {main} thrown in **C:\Abyss Web Server\htdocs\uncaught.php** on line **8**

The key to handling exceptions is to anticipate the error by trying to execute an action within a **try** code block, and determine how the script should proceed in an associated **catch** code block. The catching block is passed an **Exception** class object that has **getMessage()**, **getFile()** and **getLine()** methods to retrieve details.

An instance of the **Exception** class can be created using the **new** keyword, and can be explicitly thrown using the **throw** keyword.

A custom exception handler can also be created as a derived class of the **Exception** class, to provide your own custom methods:

exception.php

1 Begin a PHP script by defining a function that will throw an exception when a conditional test fails

```php
<?php
function check_size( $num )
{
  if( $num < 10 )
  { throw new
  Exception( "Number : $num<br>Value must exceed 10" ) ; }
}
```

2 Anticipate a specific error and report the exception

```php
try { check_size( 5 ) ; }
catch( Exception $e )
{       echo '<b>Size Exception!</b><br>'.
        $e->getMessage().'<hr>' ;               }
```

...cont'd

3 Next, create a custom exception handler class

```php
class CustomException extends Exception
{
  public function get_details()
  {
    $details = 'File : '.$this->getFile().
    '<br>Line : '.$this->getLine().
    '<br>'.$this->getMessage() ;
    return $details ;
  }
}
```

For more on derived classes and inheritance see page 116.

4 Now, add another function that will throw an exception when a conditional test fails

```php
function check_parity( $num )
{
  if( $num % 2 !== 0 )
  {
    throw new CustomException( "Number :
              $num<br>Value must be even" ) ;
  }
}
```

5 Finally, anticipate a specific error and report the exception

```php
try { check_parity( 5 ) ; }
catch( CustomException $e )
{ echo '<b>Parity Exception!</b><br>'.
      $e->get_details().'<hr>' ;               }
```

A **try** block can contain multiple **throw** statements to anticipate multiple error conditions, and can be followed by multiple **catch** blocks to handle those exceptions.

6 Save the document in your web server's **/htdocs** directory as **exception.php** then open the page via HTTP to see the exceptions caught and appropriate message details

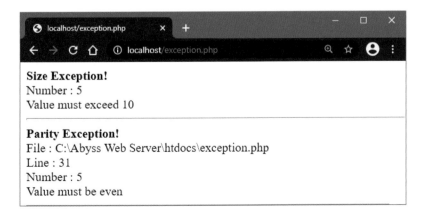

135

Summary

- The **fopen()** function is used to create a filestream object and requires two arguments to specify a file name and a file mode.

- It is good practice to provide an alternative with the **die()** function in case an attempt to create a filestream fails.

- The **fread()** function is used to read a filestream created using the 'r' file mode, and the **filesize()** function can be used to specify the byte size of the file.

- Upon completion of any file operation, the filestream must be destroyed by calling the **fclose()** function.

- The **fgets()** function can be used to read a file line-by-line, and the **feof()** function can recognize the end of a file.

- The **fgetc()** function can be used to read a file character-by-character and will return false at the end of the file.

- Text can be written into a file by specifying the filestream and the file name as arguments to the **fwrite()** function.

- The **fwrite()** function will overwrite existing text using the 'w' file mode but will append text when using the 'a' file mode.

- The name of a function can be specified as the argument to the **set_error_handler()** function to nominate it as a custom error handler.

- The error handler function is called when an error occurs or can be called explicitly using the **trigger_error()** function.

- An exception is thrown when a specific error condition occurs.

- If an exception is not caught, PHP will treat it as a fatal error and issue an Uncaught Exception message.

- A **try** code block is used to anticipate a specific error, and its associated **catch** block is used to determine how the script should proceed when that error occurs.

- An **Exception** class object has **getMessage()**, **getFile()** and **getLine()** methods that can retrieve exception details.

- A custom exception handler can be created as a derived class of the **Exception** class to provide custom exception methods.

9 Producing forms

This chapter demonstrates **138** Performing actions

how to use PHP scripts to **140** Checking set values

process HTML form data. **142** Validating form data

144 Filtering data

146 Sending hidden data

148 Handling submissions

150 Making sticky forms

152 Uploading files

154 Surrounding forms

156 Appending link data

158 Summary

Performing actions

Processing data submitted from an HTML form on a web page is perhaps the most fundamental task performed by a PHP script.

The HTML **<form>** tag's **action** attribute is used to nominate the PHP script that will process ("handle") the form data. Additionally, the **<form>** tag's **method** attribute is used to specify how the data is sent to the script – typically by the **POST** method. So the HTML form tag and attributes might look like this:

<form action="script.php" method="POST">

PHP provides a special "superglobal" **$_POST** array variable in which it stores form data submitted by the **POST** method. It creates an array element of the same name as each submitted form element name, storing the value they contain. For example, with this form element:

<input type="text" name="email" >

On submission of the form, PHP will create an array element named **$_POST['email']** containing the value entered into that form input by the user.

For easy recognition, PHP variables of the same names as the form elements can be assigned the values stored in their corresponding **$_POST** array elements. The values can then be displayed in a response page created by the action handler script:

action.php

 Create an HTML document containing a form with three text input fields for data submission
```
<form action="action_handler.php" method="POST">
<dl>
<dt>Name:
<dd><input type="text" name="name">
<dt>Email Address:
<dd><input type="text" name="mail">
<dt>Comments:
<dd><textarea rows="5" cols="20" name="comment" >
</textarea>
</dl>
<p><input type="submit" ></p>
</form>
```

 Now, save the document in your web server's **/htdocs** directory as **action.php**

...cont'd

3 Next, create an HTML document containing a script to assign form values to like-named PHP variables for output

```php
<?php
$name = $_POST['name'] ;
$mail = $_POST['mail'] ;
$comment = $_POST['comment'] ;
echo "<p>Thanks for this comment $name ...</p>" ;
echo "<p><i>$comment</i></p>" ;
echo "<p>We will reply to $mail</p>" ;
?>
```

action_handler.php

4 Save the document in your web server's **/htdocs** directory as **action_handler.php** then open **action.php** via HTTP and submit some data to see it get displayed in the response page produced by the PHP script

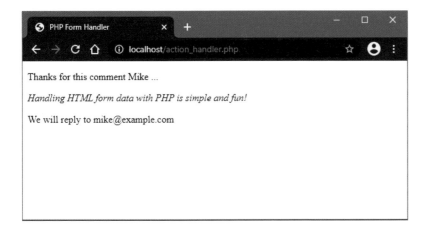

Hot tip

Form submission methods may be either "GET" or "POST". The **GET** method appends name=value pairs to the URL but is mostly used to request information – such as retrieving a database record. The **POST** method can submit more data, is more secure as the data is not appended to the URL, and is mostly used when an action is to be performed – such as updating a database record. The **POST** method is therefore preferred for most examples in this book.

Checking set values

PHP can easily ensure that the user has entered data into submitted HTML form fields using the built-in **isset()** function. This function takes the name of a variable as its argument and returns **TRUE** only if that variable value is not **NULL** – thus ensuring that the variable has been "set" with some value. Empty form fields will be **NULL** unless the user has entered a value.

Conditional tests can be made with the **isset()** function to indicate where form fields have been left empty, or to provide a response page where the fields have been completed:

isset.php

1 Create an HTML document containing a form with three radio buttons providing a single field for data submission

```
<form action="isset_handler.php" method="POST">
<fieldset>
<legend>What kind of language is PHP?</legend>
Scripting<input type="radio"
        name="definition" value="Scripting"> <br>
Markup<input type="radio"
        name="definition" value="Markup"> <br>
Programming<input type="radio"
        name="definition" value="Programming">
</fieldset><p><input type="submit" ></p>
</form>
```

2 Now, save the document in your web server's **/htdocs** directory as **isset.php**

isset_handler.php

3 Next, create an HTML document containing a PHP script to initialize a variable with a submitted value – or with **NULL** if no value has been submitted

```
<?php

if ( isset( $_POST['definition'] ) )
{
  $definition = $_POST['definition'] ;
}
else
{
  $definition = NULL ;
}

# Response statements to be inserted here (Step 4).

?>
```

...cont'd

4 Finally, insert statements to output an appropriate response according to the value of the variable

```
if ( $definition != NULL )
{
  if ( $definition != 'Scripting' )
  { echo "$definition is Incorrect" ; }
  else
  { echo "$definition is Correct" ; }
}
else
{ echo 'You must select one answer' ; }
?>
```

Hot tip

It is technically more efficient to test whether a condition is not **TRUE** than whether it is **TRUE** – as fewer possibilities need evaluating.

5 Save the document in your web server's **/htdocs** directory as **isset_handler.php** then open **isset.php** via HTTP and submit the form to see the responses

Validating form data

As users may inadvertently submit forms with empty fields, or with data in the wrong format, it is essential your PHP scripts ensure required fields are completed and submitted data is valid.

To ensure the user has entered something into a text field, PHP provides an **empty()** function that accepts a variable argument and returns **TRUE** if its value is an empty string, zero, **NULL** or **FALSE**.

To ensure the user has entered data in numeric format, PHP provides an **is_numeric()** function that accepts a variable argument and returns **TRUE** only if its value is a number.

More specific data validation can be performed using the PHP **preg_match()** function that accepts a "regular expression" argument and a variable argument in which to seek a pattern. Typically, this is used to ensure an email address is in the expected format:

valid.php

 Create an HTML document containing a form with two text fields for data submission

```
<form action="valid_handler.php" method="POST">
<fieldset>
<legend>Enter a quantity and email address</legend>
<p>Quantity : <input type="text" name="quantity"></p>
<p>Email Address : <input type="text" name="email"></p>
</fieldset><p><input type="submit" ></p>
</form>
```

Now, save the document in your web server's **/htdocs** directory as **valid.php**

valid_handler.php

Next, create an HTML document containing a PHP script to initialize a variable with a submitted value – or with **NULL** if no value has been submitted

```
<?php
if ( !empty ( $_POST['quantity'] ) )
{
  $quantity = $_POST['quantity'] ;
  # Format validation to be inserted here (Step 4).
}
else
{ $quantity = NULL ; echo 'You must enter a quantity<br>' ; }
```

 Insert statements to ensure the format is numeric

```
if ( !is_numeric( $quantity ) )
{ $quantity = NULL ; echo 'Quantity must be numeric<br>' ; }
```

5 Now, add statements to initialize another variable with a submitted value – or with **NULL** if no value is submitted

```
if ( !empty ( $_POST['email'] ) )
{
  $email = $_POST['email'] ;
  # Format validation to be inserted here (Step 6).
}
else
{ $email = NULL ; echo 'You must enter an email address' ; }
```

6 Next, insert statements to ensure the email address uses the expected pattern

```
$pattern = '/\b[\w.-]+@[\w.-]+\.[A-Za-z]{2,6}\b/' ;
if ( !preg_match( $pattern , $email ) )
{ $email = NULL ; echo 'Email address is incorrect format' ; }
```

Hot tip

Strictly speaking, the topic of regular expressions is outside the remit of this book, but you can precisely copy the pattern in this example to ensure email addresses are in the expected format.

7 Finally, add a statement to output valid submitted data

```
 if ( ( $quantity != NULL ) && ( $email != NULL ) )
{ echo "Email : $email<br>Quantity : $quantity " ; }
?>
```

8 Save the document in your web server's **/htdocs** directory as **valid_handler.php** then open **valid.php** via HTTP and submit the form to see the responses

143

Filtering data

To validate user input easily, PHP provides a **filter_var()** function that can be used to both validate and "sanitize" input values. This function requires two arguments to specify the variable to be filtered and a constant name of the filter to be used:

Filter Constant Name	Convention
FILTER_VALIDATE_BOOLEAN	Boolean value
FILTER_VALIDATE_EMAIL	Email address format
FILTER_VALIDATE_FLOAT	Floating-point number
FILTER_VALIDATE_INT	Integer number
FILTER_VALIDATE_IP	IP address format
FILTER_VALIDATE_MAC	MAC address format
FILTER_VALIDATE_REGEXP	Regular expression format
FILTER_VALIDATE_URL	URL format
FILTER_SANITIZE_EMAIL	Strip invalid characters
FILTER_SANITIZE_ENCODED	URL-encode string
FILTER_SANITIZE_MAGIC_QUOTES	Backslash-escape characters
FILTER_SANITIZE_NUMBER_FLOAT	Strip all non-digits
FILTER_SANITIZE_NUMBER_INT	Strip all non-digits
FILTER_SANITIZE_SPECIAL_CHARS	HTML-escape '"<>&
FILTER_SANITIZE_STRING	Strip HTML tags
FILTER_SANITIZE_URL	Strip invalid characters
FILTER_CALLBACK	Call a custom filter function

The validation filters return **TRUE** when validation succeeds, otherwise they will return **FALSE**.

Some filters allow further options to be specified. For example, a numeric range can be specified to **FILTER_VALIDATE_INT**.

...cont'd

PHP

filter.php

1 Create an HTML document containing a PHP script that begins by writing a styled HTML page heading
```php
<?php
$hdr = '<h1 style="color:red">PHP in easy steps</h1>' ;
echo $hdr ;
```

2 Next, sanitize the page heading by stripping the HTML tags to remove styling and display the stripped version
```php
$hdr = filter_var( $hdr , FILTER_SANITIZE_STRING ) ;
echo "Sanitized heading : $hdr" ;
```

3 Now, add a function to validate a parameter as being a correctly formatted email address
```php
function validate( $email )
{
  if ( filter_var( $email , FILTER_VALIDATE_EMAIL ) )
  { echo( "<hr>$email IS a valid email address" ) ; }
  else
  { echo( "<hr>$email IS NOT a valid email address" ); }
}
```

4 Create an email address containing an illegal space and attempt validation, then sanitize the email address and attempt validation once more
```php
$email = 'mike @example.com' ;
validate( $email ) ;
$email = filter_var( $email , FILTER_SANITIZE_EMAIL ) ;
validate( $email ) ;
?>
```

Submitted user input can break your webpage so should always be validated.

5 Save the document in your web server's **/htdocs** directory as **filter.php** then open it via HTTP to see filtration

Sending hidden data

In addition to data entered by the user into HTML form input fields, data generated by PHP can be submitted using HTML hidden form fields. Like regular input fields these also send a name=value pair to the form handler script, but here the value is supplied by PHP, not by the user.

Typically, data submitted using hidden form fields might include the login name of the user and a timestamp of the submission:

 Create an HTML document containing a PHP script to define the timezone and initialize two variables

```php
<?php
date_default_timezone_set( 'UTC' ) ;
$time = date( ' H:i , F j ' ) ;
$user = 'Mike' ;
```

 Now, add a statement to write a complete form containing a regular input field and two hidden fields, whose values are set by the variables

```php
echo '
<form action="hidden_handler.php" method="POST">
<fieldset>
<legend>Send us your comments</legend>
<textarea rows="5" cols="20" name="comment">
</textarea>
<input type="hidden" name="user" value=" '. $user .' ">
<input type="hidden" name="time" value=" '. $time.' ">
</fieldset><p><input type="submit" ></p></form> ' ;
?>
```

 Save the document in your web server's **/htdocs** directory as **hidden.php**

Next, create an HTML document containing a PHP script to initialize a variable with a submitted value – or with **NULL** if no value has been submitted

```php
<?php
if ( !empty ( $_POST['comment'] ) )
{
  $comment = $_POST['comment'] ;
}
else
{
  $comment = NULL ; echo 'You must enter a comment' ;
}
```

PHP

hidden.php

Beware

The timestamp in this example is created when the form gets created, not when the form gets submitted.

PHP

hidden_handler.php

…cont'd

5 Now, add statements to initialize two variables if the hidden form field values have been set
```
$time =
( !isset ( $_POST['time'] ) ) ? NULL : $_POST['time'] ;

$user =
( !isset ( $_POST['user'] ) ) ? NULL : $_POST['user'] ;
```

Hot tip

Notice the ternary **? :** operator is used here in place of a more lengthy **if else** statement.

6 Finally, add a statement to output valid submitted data
```
if ( ( $comment != NULL )  &&
                ( $time != NULL ) && ( $user != NULL )  )
{ echo "<p>Comment received : \" $comment \"<br>
                From $user at $time </p>" ;  }

?>
```

7 Save the document in your web server's **/htdocs** directory as **hidden_handler.php** then open **hidden.php** via HTTP and submit the form to see the responses

Don't forget

You can include quotes in output by prefixing them with a backslash to escape them from recognition – as demonstrated here.

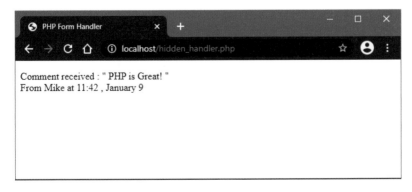

Handling submissions

The examples so far in this chapter have each used two documents – one to display an HTML form and another to handle the form submission. This procedure can, however, be performed by a single document, using a simple technique to determine whether a form should be displayed or its submission should be handled.

PHP provides a special "superglobal" **$_SERVER** array variable with a **REQUEST_METHOD** element in which it stores the type of request. Where a form uses the **POST** method for submission, two different types of request are made to the PHP script when the page loads – simply displaying the form uses the standard **GET** method made by most web pages, whereas submitting the form uses the **POST** method. Therefore, the request method can be examined to determine which course of action to take.

Using this technique, the name of the same single page is also specified as the form handler to the HTML **action** attribute. The form can be displayed by the usual **echo** instruction, and validation checks can be made for the response in the same way as described for separate form handler scripts:

single.php

1 Create an HTML document containing a PHP script that examines the page request method

```php
<?php
if ( $_SERVER[ 'REQUEST_METHOD' ] != 'POST' )
{
  # Form display statements to be inserted here (Step 2).
}
else
{
  # Form handling statements to be inserted here (Step 3).
}
```

2 Now, insert a statement to display a form when the page has been requested by the standard **GET** method

```php
 echo '
<form action="single.php" method="POST">
<fieldset>
<legend>Send us your comments</legend>
<textarea rows="5" cols="40" name="comment">
</textarea>
</fieldset>
<p><input type="submit" ></p>
</form> ' ;
```

3 Next, insert a statement to handle the form submission when the page has been requested by the **POST** method

```php
if ( !empty ( $_POST['comment'] ) )
{
  $comment = $_POST['comment'] ;
  echo "Comment : $comment " ;
}
else
{ $comment = NULL ; echo 'You must enter a comment' ; }
?>
```

Hot tip

The form will be handled by the same page on submission if the action attribute specifies an empty string **action=""** – but it is preferable to specify the page name.

4 Save the document in your web server's **/htdocs** directory as **single.php** then submit the form to see the responses

Making sticky forms

When a user attempts to submit a form where a required field has not been completed, it is desirable to retain the entries in the fields they have completed, by making the form "sticky". This is especially so for lengthy forms with many fields – so the user need not complete all fields once more – and is easily achieved with PHP.

Simply assigning the relevant submitted field data from the **$_POST** array to the HTML tag's **value** attribute with **echo** retains the entry when the form is displayed again for completion. As a precaution, the statement should use the **isset()** function to check that the field was in fact completed before submission.

An error message for each incomplete field can be assigned to an array to advise of omissions when the form is displayed again, or a message written confirming success when all fields are completed:

PHP

sticky.php

Hot tip

$_SERVER['PHP_SELF'] is used by this example to ensure the script will still work if renamed.

Don't forget

The **if** statement tests that the form has been submitted by checking the request method is **POST**, not the **GET** method that is used to display the empty form.

1 Create an HTML document containing a sticky form with two text fields for name and email address details

```
<form method="POST"
        action="<?php $_SERVER[ 'PHP_SELF' ] ?>" >
<p>Name:
<input type="text" name="name"
        value="<?php if ( isset( $_POST[ 'name' ] ) )
                echo $_POST[ 'name' ] ; ?>"> </p>
<p>Email:
<input type="text" name="email"
        value="<?php if ( isset( $_POST[ 'email' ] ) )
                echo $_POST[ 'email' ] ; ?>"></p>
<p><input type="submit"></p>
</form>
```

2 Now, add a PHP script to handle the form submission

```
<?php

if ( $_SERVER[ 'REQUEST_METHOD' ] == 'POST' )
{
  // Statements to be inserted here (Steps 3-5).
}

?>
```

3 Next, insert into the PHP script block a statement to create an array for error messages

```
$errors = array() ;
```

Then, insert statements to initialize variables with submitted values, or add to the errors array for omissions

```
if ( empty( $_POST[ 'name' ] ) ) { $errors[] = 'name' ; }
else { $name = trim( $_POST[ 'name' ] ) ; }

if ( empty( $_POST[ 'email' ] ) ) { $errors[] = 'email' ; }
else { $email = trim( $_POST[ 'email' ] ) ; }
```

 Now, insert statements to write error messages or confirm successful form submission

```
if( !empty( $errors ) )
{ echo 'Error! Please enter your  ' ;
   foreach ( $errors as $msg ) { echo " - $msg " ; } }
else { echo "Success! Thanks $name " ; }
```

6 Save the document in your web server's **/htdocs** directory as **sticky.php** then open it via HTTP and submit the form to see the retained values and response messages

Hot tip

It is good practice to use the **trim()** function, as seen here, to remove any leading and trailing spaces from the submitted field value.

151

Uploading files

The PHP **$_FILES** superglobal variable makes it simple to **POST** file uploads from an HTML form if the **<form>** tag includes an **enctype** attribute set to "multipart/formdata". When submitted, a **$_FILES** associative array is created with keys that include the file **name**, a generated temporary name (**tmp_name**), and the file **size**. The filename and size can be used for validation. The temporary filename can then be specified to the **move_uploaded_file()** function along with the original filename to upload the file:

upload.php

1. Create an HTML document containing a sticky form with a file type input named "image"

```
<form action="<?php $_SERVER[ 'PHP_SELF' ] ?>"
    method="POST"  enctype = "multipart/formdata" >
Select an image to upload :
<input type="file" name="image" >
<input type="submit" value="Upload Image"> </form>
```

Beware

The PHP configuration must permit file uploads for this example to work. The configuration file **php.ini**, within the PHP directory, must contain a line **file_uploads = On**.

2. Now, add a PHP script to handle the form submission

```
<?php

if ( $_SERVER[ 'REQUEST_METHOD' ] == 'POST' )
{
    // Statements to be inserted here (Steps 3-7).
}

?>
```

3. Next, insert statements to initialize three variables with information about the file selected by the user

```
$name = $_FILES[ 'image' ][ 'name' ] ;
$temp = $_FILES[ 'image' ][ 'tmp_name' ] ;
$size = $_FILES[ 'image' ][ 'size' ] ;
```

Hot tip

Notice how the **pathinfo()** function provides the file extension part of the filename here.

4. Now, insert statements to ensure the selected file is of a desired file type by testing the file extension, or quit

```
$ext = pathinfo( $name , PATHINFO_EXTENSION ) ;
$ext = strtolower( $ext ) ;
if( $ext != 'png' && $ext != 'jpg' && $ext != 'gif' )
{ echo 'Format must be PNG, JPG, or GIF' ; exit() ; }
```

5. Insert a statement to ensure the selected file is of a desired file size, or quit

```
if( $size > 512000 )
{ echo 'File size must not exceed 500Kb' ; exit() ; }
```

6 Insert a statement to ensure the selected file does not have the same name as one already on the server, or quit

```
if( file_exists( $name ) )
{ echo 'File '.$name.' already uploaded' ; exit() ; }
```

7 Finally, attempt to upload the file, naming it by its original filename and displaying it below the form

```
try
{
  move_uploaded_file( $temp , $name ) ;
  echo 'File uploaded : '.$name ;
  echo '<br><img src="'.$name.'">' ;
}
catch( Exception $e )
{
  echo 'File upload failed!' ;
}
```

Hot tip

The arguments to the **move_uploaded_file()** function specify the (temporary) filename and destination. It could usefully specify a dedicated directory path destination, such as **'uploads/'.$name**.

8 Save the document in your web server's **/htdocs** directory as **upload.php** then open it via HTTP and select a suitable image file for upload to the **/htdocs** directory

coke.png

Surrounding forms

PHP usefully allows multiple files to be incorporated together to create a single web page. This means that dynamic forms can be surrounded by static header and footer content that can be easily reused to create other pages within a website.

The PHP **include()** function takes the URL of another file to be incorporated within a web page as its argument. Typically, included static content files are HTML and are located in an "includes" folder within the **/htdocs** directory of your web server.

PHP also provides a **require()** function that works just like the **include()** function to incorporate other files within a web page, but is subtly different. When the **include()** function fails, as the specified file cannot be found, for example, a warning gets sent to the browser but the script continues to run. When the **require()** function fails, an error is printed but the script gets halted. Usually, the **include()** function incorporates static HTML files, whereas the **require()** function incorporates dynamic PHP scripts.

Importantly, the title of a web page incorporating multiple files can be dynamically written by PHP to allow maximum flexibility of otherwise static HTML header content:

header.html

1 Create an HTML document containing static header content and a PHP snippet to write the page title

```
<!DOCTYPE HTML>
<html lang="en">
<head>
<meta charset="UTF-8">
<title> <?php echo $page_title ; ?> </title>
<link rel="stylesheet" href="includes/style.css">
</head>

<body>
<header><h1>Page Header</h1></header>
```

footer.html

2 Now, create an HTML document containing footer content

```
<footer><p>Page Footer</p></footer>
</body>
</html>
```

3 Next, create a folder named "includes" in the **/htdocs** directory of your web server and save the above documents inside it as **header.html** and **footer.html** respectively

...cont'd

4 Create a CSS style sheet to present the header and footer content (and rules to present aspects of later examples)

```css
header > h1 { border-bottom : 1px dashed black ;
              font-style : italic ; font-size : x-large ; }
footer > p { border-top : 1px dashed black ;
                            font-style : italic ; }
table { border-spacing : 5px ; width : 530px ; }
th { color : #FFF ; background : #000 ; text-align : left ; }
td { border-bottom : 1px solid black ;
         padding : 3px ; background : #F0F0F0 ;
         text-align : left ; vertical-align :top ; }
p#err_msg { color : #F00 ; font-weight : bold ; }
```

style.css

5 Save the style sheet in the **/includes** folder you have created, alongside the HTML header and footer files

6 Finally, create a PHP script that sets the web page title and surrounds a form with header and footer content

```php
<?php
$page_title = 'PHP Include' ;
include ( 'includes/header.html' ) ;
echo '<form action="include.php" method="POST">
<p>Name: <input type="text" name="name"> </p>
<p>Email: <input type="text" name="email" ></p>
<p><input type="submit"></p></form>' ;
include ( 'includes/footer.html' ) ;
?>
```

include.php

7 Save the PHP script in your web server's **/htdocs** directory as **include.php** then open it via HTTP to see the page title set and a form surrounded by static content

PHP Include — localhost/include.php

Page Header

Name: [   ]

Email: [   ]

[Submit]

Page Footer

Hot tip

You can use your browser's View Source facility to see that the entire content has been effectively incorporated into a single web page.

Appending link data

PHP predefined "superglobal" variables, such as the **$_SERVER** array variable that stores the page request method and the **$_SESSION** array variable that stores user data across pages of a website until the user quits, are accessible in all scopes of any script.

Where an HTML form submits data using the **POST** method, the **$_POST** array stores the value of submitted form values in like-named array elements. So, the value of a submitted field named "city" can be accessed using **$_POST['city']**.

Similarly, where data is submitted using the **GET** method, the **$_GET** array stores the value of submitted values in named array elements. So the value of a submitted data named "id" can be accessed using **$_GET['id']**. This is typically used to submit data to a script by appending a name=value pair to the URL in an HTML hyperlink anchor, like this:

<a href="www.example.com/script.php?id=1">

The script receiving the data, nominated by the hyperlink, may then use the passed value to determine a response:

The **$_SESSION** superglobal will be used to store user details in Chapter 10.

link.php

 Create an HTML document containing a PHP script that seeks an element named "id" within the **$_GET** array
```php
<?php
if ( isset ( $_GET[ 'id' ] )
{
  # Handler statements to be inserted here (Steps 2-3).
}
```

 Next, insert a handler statement to assign a passed value to a like-named PHP variable
```php
$id = $_GET[ 'id' ] ;
```

3 Now, insert a handler statement to output an appropriate response according to the value passed
```php
switch( $id )
{
  case 1 : echo 'Cow selected<hr>' ; break ;
  case 2 : echo 'Dog selected<hr>' ; break ;
  case 3 : echo 'Goat selected<hr>' ; break ;
}
```

4 Finally, add statements to display hyperlinks with appended values

```
echo '<h1>Select a buddy</h1>' ;
echo ' <p><a href="link.php?id=1">Cow</a> |' ;
echo ' <a href="link.php?id=2">Dog</a> | ' ;
echo ' <a href="link.php?id=3">Goat</a></p>' ;
?>
```

5 Save the PHP script in your web server's **/htdocs** directory as **link.php** then open it via HTTP and click the links to see the responses for the passed values

PHP also provides a **$_REQUEST** superglobal that contains the entire contents of the **$_POST** and **$_GET** arrays. This means that **$_POST['city']** is also accessible using **$_REQUEST['city']** but this should be avoided. Always use the specific array for the type of submission instead.

Notice that the passed name=value pair is visible in the browser address field.

Summary

- An HTML <form> tag's **action** attribute specifies the PHP script to handle the form submission, and its **method** attribute specifies how the data is sent to the script.

- Form data submitted by the **POST** method gets automatically stored in the PHP superglobal **$_POST** array variable.

- Elements of the **$_POST** array are named the same as the HTML form element containing each submitted value.

- PHP can ensure that the user has entered data into submitted HTML form fields using the built-in **isset()** function.

- The PHP **empty()** function checks whether a value has been entered into a form text field.

- Format validation can be performed on submitted form data by the **is_numeric()** function and **preg_match()** function.

- Data generated by PHP, such as a timestamp created by the **date()** function, can be submitted from hidden form fields.

- The PHP superglobal **$_SERVER['REQUEST_METHOD']** array element stores the type of request made to load the page.

- Sticky forms retain their field data simply by writing any submitted values back to the HTML input's **value** attribute.

- The PHP **include()** and **require()** functions are used to incorporate other content and scripts within a web page.

- Data submitted by the **GET** method gets automatically stored in the PHP superglobal **$_GET** array variable.

- Hyperlinks can have name=value pairs appended to submit data to a script using the **GET** method.

10 Preserving data

This chapter demonstrates   **160**   Submitting cookie data

how to preserve data using   **161**   Setting cookies

cookies and PHP sessions.   **162**   Getting cookies

164   Viewing cookie data

166   Submitting session data

167   Setting sessions

168   Getting sessions

170   Viewing session data

172   Summary

Submitting cookie data

Data entered by a user is frequently required across multiple pages of a website. User data can conveniently be stored in small "cookie" files on the client machine, so the user need not tediously enter the same data repeatedly. The PHP **setcookie()** function makes it easy to create a cookie by specifying three arguments:

setcookie(*name* **,** *value* **,** *expiry-time* **) ;**

When an HTML form is submitted to the server using the **POST** method, its field data is automatically assigned to the special PHP **$_POST** global array variable. A script can check for the presence of individual submission fields using a built-in PHP **isset()** function to seek an element of a specified HTML field name. When this confirms the field is indeed present, its name and value can usefully be stored in a cookie. This might be used to store username and password details for use across a website:

The **setcookie()** function can also accept arguments to specify visible path, domain, https security, and visibility for http access.

cookie_form.html

1 Create an HTML document and add this form to its body section, specifying submission method and the name of a PHP submission-handler script

```
<form name = "entry" method = "POST"
                        action = "cookie_set.php">
<fieldset>
<legend>Enter Only AlphaNumeric Characters</legend>
Name : <input type = "text" name = "user" >
Password : <input type = "password" name = "pass" >
<br><br><input type = "submit" value = "Log In" >
</fieldset>
</form>
```

2 Save the document in your web server's **/htdocs** directory as **cookie_form.html** then open the page via HTTP to see the form

Storing passwords in cookies is not the most secure method but is used here merely to demonstrate how to use cookies to store data.

160

Setting cookies

Upon receiving a form submission, a PHP script can check for the presence of fields and might perform validation of their associated values. For example, the **ctype_alnum()** function could be used to simply confirm that the values only contain alphanumeric data.

Once validated, the **setcookie()** function can store the submitted fields' names and values. Additionally, a hash conversion could be made of password values using the **md5()** function. On successful completion, the script can then relocate the browser to another page using the **header()** function to specify that page's URL:

The **ctype_alnum()** function returns true only if its argument contains alphanumeric characters.

1. Begin a PHP script with a function to handle failed validation attempts

```php
<?php
function reject( $entry )
{
  echo "Invalid $entry <br>" ;
  echo 'Please <a href="cookie_form.html">Log In</a>' ;
  exit() ;
}
```

cookie_set.php

2. Next, add a conditional test block to set two cookies for valid data, or call the function to handle failed attempts

```php
if( isset( $_POST[ 'user' ] ) )
{
  $user = trim( $_POST[ 'user' ] ) ;
  if( !ctype_alnum( $user ) ) { reject( 'User Name' ) ; }

  if( isset( $_POST[ 'pass' ] ) )
  {
    $pass = trim( $_POST[ 'pass' ] ) ;
    if( !ctype_alnum( $pass ) ) { reject( 'Password' ) ; }
    else
    {
      setcookie( 'user' , $user , time()+3600 ) ;
      setcookie( 'pass' , md5( $pass ) , time()+3600 ) ;
      header( 'Location: cookie_get.php' ) ;
    }
  }
}
else { header( 'Location: cookie_form.html' ) ; }
?>
```

Notice how the **time()** function is used here to get the current time, then one hour is added (in seconds) to set the cookie expiration time one hour ahead.

3. Save the document in your web server's **/htdocs** directory as **cookie_set.php** then see pages 162-163 for how to retrieve the stored cookie data

The final **else** statement will relocate to the HTML form page if the script URL is opened directly.

Getting cookies

Once cookies are set, they are automatically assigned to the special PHP **$_COOKIE** global array variable. A script can check for the presence of an individual cookie using the built-in PHP **isset()** function to seek a cookie of a specified name. When this confirms the cookie is indeed present, its value can usefully be assigned to a regular script variable. This might be used to retrieve a stored username for output on a page. Where a sought cookie is absent, the script can offer an alternative to the user:

cookie_get.php

1 Begin a PHP script with a test to find a cookie and retrieve data for output upon success

```php
<?php
if( isset( $_COOKIE[ 'user' ] ) )
{
  $user = $_COOKIE[ 'user' ] ;
  echo "<h1>Welcome $user !</h1><hr>" ;
  echo '<a href="cookie_data.php">View Cookie</a>' ;
}
```

2 Next, add alternative output for when the cookie is absent

```php
else
{
  echo 'Please <a href="cookie_form.html">Log In</a>' ;
}
?>
```

3 Save the document in your web server's **/htdocs** directory as **cookie_get.php**

4 Now, open the HTML form **cookie_form.html** (created on page 160) via HTTP and push the submit button to see the login attempt fail validation, so no cookies are set

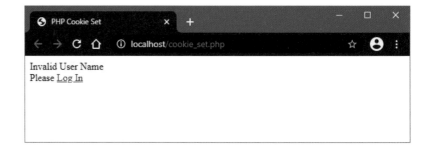

...cont'd

⑤ Click the hyperlink to return to the HTML form and enter a valid username, then push the submit button to see the login attempt fail validation again

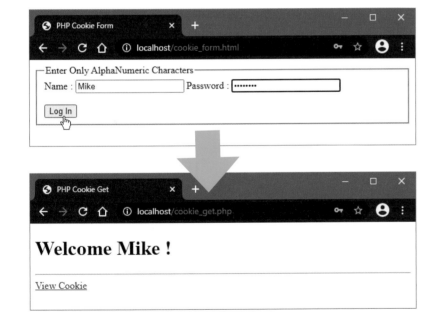

⑥ Return to the HTML form once more and enter a valid username and password to see validation succeed

⑦ See pages 164-165 for how to view data stored within cookies, using the **cookie_data.php** target of the hyperlink seen above

Don't forget

You can also return to the HTML form and enter a username or a password that includes non-alphanumeric characters, to see validation fail again.

Hot tip

Validation could be extended. For example, it may also allow underscore characters and might specify a minimum permissible password length.

163

Viewing cookie data

The special PHP **$_COOKIE** global array variable stores cookie names and values in an associative array of keys and values. Stored content can be viewed by looping through the array to see all names and values, or by using the PHP **var_dump()** function:

cookie_data.php

Hot tip

You can call the **setcookie( )** function at any time to create a new cookie or overwrite an existing cookie.

1 Begin a PHP script with a test to find if any cookies are set and retrieve all stored names and values upon success

```php
<?php
if( count( $_COOKIE ) > 0 )
{
  echo '<dl> ' ;
  foreach( $_COOKIE as $key => $value )
  {
    echo "<dt>Key: $key" ;
    echo "<dd>Value: $value" ;
  }
  echo '</dl><hr>' ;
  var_dump( $_COOKIE ) ;
}
```

2 Next, add alternative output for when cookies are absent

```php
else
{
  echo 'Please <a href="cookie_form.html">Log In</a>' ;
}
?>
```

3 Save the document in your web server's **/htdocs** directory as **cookie_data.php**

4 Now, open the HTML form **cookie_form.html** (page 160) via HTTP and enter valid login data, then follow the link on **cookie_get.php** (page 162) to see cookie data

Key: user
    Value: Mike
Key: pass
    Value: a6b7bcfe6f5fadff8ea572c84edb6207

array(2) { ["user"]=> string(4) "Mike" ["pass"]=> string(32)
"a6b7bcfe6f5fadff8ea572c84edb6207" }

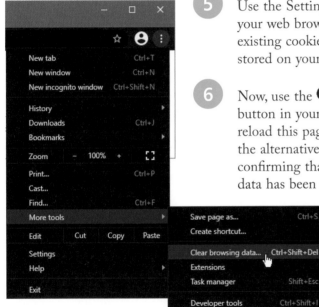

5 Use the Settings menu on your web browser to clear existing cookies that are stored on your system

6 Now, use the Refresh button in your browser to reload this page and see the alternative content – confirming that the cookie data has been removed

Hot tip

The PHP manual describes the removal of a cookie by setting its value to empty and its expiration date to the past. For example, **setcookie($_COOKIE['user'] , '' , time()-3600)**. Additionally, the **unset()** function can be used to destroy a specified variable.

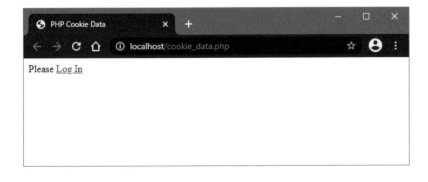

Please Log In

Submitting session data

User data can be stored in cookies on the client computer only if the user chooses to allow cookies onto their system. Many users prefer to disallow cookies, however, to avoid tracking – but PHP provides a better alternative. With PHP, user data can be stored on the server using the special **$_SESSION** global array variable. In order for PHP sessions to work, each PHP page must call the built-in **session_start()** function at the top of the page – before any HTML tags! HTML form submissions to the server via the **POST** method assigns field data to the special PHP **$_POST** global array variable, and individual submission fields can be sought using the built-in PHP **isset()** function. When this confirms the field is present, its name and value can be stored in a session variable. This might be used to store username and password details for use across a website, as an alternative to cookie storage:

session_form.html

1 Create an HTML document and add this form to its body section, specifying submission method and the name of a PHP submission-handler script

```
<form name = "entry" method = "POST"
                            action = "session_set.php">
<fieldset>
<legend>For Name : Enter Only Letters</legend>
Name : <input type="text" name="user" >
Password : <input type="password" name="pass" >
<p>For Password : Enter Only A-Z a-z 0-9 . _ (Minimum 8
Characters)</p> <input type="submit" value="Log In">
</fieldset>
</form>
```

2 Save the document in your web server's **/htdocs** directory as **session_form.html** then open the page via HTTP to see the form

Session variables will only be accessible to a PHP script if the **session_start()** function has been called at the top of the page.

PHP Session Form

localhost/session_form.html

For Name : Enter Only Letters

Name : [   ]   Password : [   ]

For Password : Enter Only A-Z a-z 0-9 . _ (Minimum 8 Characters)

[Log In]

Setting sessions

Upon receiving a form submission, a PHP script can check for the presence of fields and might perform validation of their associated values. For example, the **ctype_alpha()** function could be used to confirm they contain only letters, and the **preg_match()** function could be used to confirm a value matches a specified pattern. Once validated, the submitted fields' names and values can be assigned to elements of the **$_SESSION** global array variable. On successful completion, the script can relocate the browser to the next page using the **header()** function to specify that page's URL:

The **ctype_alpha()** function returns true only if its argument contains letters.

session_set.php

1. Add an initial PHP script to make sessions available
```php
<?php session_start(); ?>
```

2. Begin a PHP script to handle failed validation attempts
```php
<?php
function reject( $entry )
{
  echo "Invalid $entry <br>" ;
  echo 'Please <a href="session_form.html">Log In</a>' ;
  exit() ;
}
```

3. Add a conditional test block to set two cookies for valid data, or call the function to handle failed attempts
```php
if( isset( $_POST[ 'user' ] ) )
{
  $user = trim( $_POST[ 'user' ] ) ;
  if( !ctype_alpha( $user ) ) { reject( 'User Name' ) ; }
  if( isset( $_POST[ 'pass' ] ) )
  {
    $pass = trim( $_POST[ 'pass' ] ) ;
    if( !preg_match( '/^[A-Za-z0-9._]{8,}$/' , $pass ) )
    { reject( 'Password' ) ; }
    else
    {
      $_SESSION[ 'user' ] = $user ;
      $_SESSION[ 'pass' ] = $pass ;
      header( 'Location: session_get.php' ) ;
    }
  }
} else { header( 'Location: session_form.html' ) ; }
?>
```

The **preg_match()** function accepts a regular expression and a string argument. Regular expressions are beyond the remit of this book but you can precisely copy this example to allow the permissible password pattern described on the form. The password is left unencrypted in this example, to demonstrate later that the user password meets the specified requirements.

4. Save the document in your web server's **/htdocs** directory as **session_set.php** then see pages 168-169 for how to retrieve data

Getting sessions

Session data is accessible from the special **$_SESSION** global array variable after a call is made to the **session_start()** function. The PHP **isset()** function can seek an element of a specified name. When this confirms the element is present, its value can usefully be assigned to a regular script variable. This might be used to retrieve a stored username for output on a page. Where a sought element is absent, the script can offer an alternative to the user:

session_get.php

1. Add an initial PHP script to make sessions available
```php
<?php session_start() ; ?>
```

2. Now, begin a PHP script to find a session variable and retrieve data for output upon success, or provide an alternative for when the session variable is absent
```php
<?php
if( isset( $_SESSION[ 'user' ] ) )
{
  $user = $_SESSION[ 'user' ] ;
  echo "<h1>Welcome $user !</h1><hr>" ;
  echo '<a href="session_data.php">View Session</a>' ;
}
else
{ echo 'Please <a href="session_form.html">Log In</a>' ; }
?>
```

3. Save the document in your web server's **/htdocs** directory as **session_get.php**

4. Now, open the HTML form **session_form.html** (created on page 166) via HTTP and push the submit button to see the login attempt fail validation

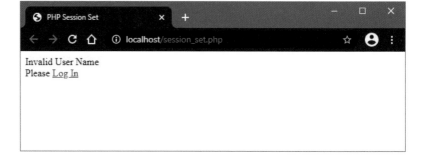

5 Return to the HTML form and submit a valid username, to see the login attempt fail validation again

You can also return to the HTML form and enter a password below the minimum length or containing invalid characters to see validation fail again.

6 Return to the HTML form once more and enter a valid username and password to see validation succeed

For Name : Enter Only Letters
Name : Susan   Password : ••••••••
For Password : Enter Only A-Z a-z 0-9 . _ (Minimum 8 Characters)
Log In

Welcome Susan !

View Session

Notice that the user in this example has added leading spaces before their name, but that's okay – these will be removed by the **trim()** function used in the **session_set.php** script.

7 See overleaf how to view data stored in session variables, using the **session_data.php** target of the link seen above

Viewing session data

The special PHP **$_SESSION** global array variable stores names and values in an associative array of keys and values. Stored content can be viewed by looping through the array to see all names and values, or by using the PHP **var_dump()** function. Additionally, each session has a unique session ID number, which can be seen using the PHP **session_id()** function.

Set session variables can be removed by specifying their element name to the PHP **unset()** function, and a session can be completely terminated by calling the **session_destroy()** function:

session_data.php

1   Add an initial PHP script to make sessions available
```php
<?php session_start(); ?>
```

2   Now, begin a PHP script to remove session variables, terminate a session, and confirm termination
```php
<?php
function kill_session()
{
  unset( $_SESSION[ 'user' ] ) ;
  unset( $_SESSION[ 'pass' ] ) ;
  session_destroy() ;
  echo '<hr>Session Destroyed<br>' ;
  echo  'Session ID : '.session_id().'<br>' ;
  var_dump( $_SESSION ) ;
}
```

3   Now, add a test to find if any session variables are set and retrieve all stored names and values
```php
if( count( $_SESSION ) > 0 )
{
  echo '<dl> ' ;
  foreach( $_SESSION as $key => $value )
  {
    echo "<dt>Key: $key" ; echo "<dd>Value: $value" ;
  }
  echo '</dl><hr>' ;
  // Statements to be inserted here (Step 4).
}
```

4   Insert statements to display the session ID and array, then call the function to terminate the session
```php
  echo 'Session ID : '.session_id().'<br>' ;
  var_dump( $_SESSION ) ;
  kill_session() ;
```

170

Don't forget

The uniqueness of each session allows variables to exist without conflict.

Hot tip

You can assign a new value to a session variable at any time to overwrite an existing stored value.

...cont'd

5 Add alternative output for when a session is absent

```
else
{ echo 'Please <a href="session_form.html">Log In</a>' ; }
?>
```

6 Save the document in your web server's **/htdocs** directory as **session_data.php**

7 Now, open the HTML form **session_form.html** (page 166) via HTTP and enter valid login data, then follow the link on **session_get.php** (page 168) to see session data

Notice that the password adheres to the permissible pattern.

8 Use the ↻ Refresh button in your browser to reload this page to see the alternative "Please Log In" content

Summary

- The PHP **set_cookie()** function can be used to store user data on the client machine for use across the pages of a website.

- There should be at least three arguments supplied to the **set_cookie()** function to specify name, value and expiry time.

- HTML form submissions via the **POST** method automatically assign field data to the PHP **$_POST** global array variable.

- The **isset()** function can seek an element of a specified HTML field name within the **$_POST** global array.

- The **ctype_alnum()** function can be used to confirm a value only contains alphanumeric data for validation.

- A hash conversion can be made of a password value using the **md5()** function for encryption.

- The PHP **header()** function can specify a Location:URL to relocate the browser.

- Once cookies are set, they are automatically assigned to the special PHP **$_COOKIE** global array variable.

- User data can be stored on the server in the PHP **$_SESSION** global array variable as an alternative to cookie storage.

- To use sessions, each PHP page must call the **session_start()** function at the top of the page before any HTML tags.

- HTML field data submitted to the **$_POST** global array can be assigned to a **$_SESSION** global variable array element.

- The **ctype_alpha()** function can be used to confirm a value only contains alphabetic letter data for validation.

- The **preg_match()** function can be used to confirm a value matches a specified pattern for validation.

- Each session has a unique session ID number, which can be seen using the PHP **session_id()** function.

- Session variables can be removed using the **unset()** function, and a session can be terminated using the **session_destroy()** function.

- Stored content can be viewed using the **var_dump()** function and by looping through the **$_COOKIE** or **$_SESSION** arrays.

11 Adding Web Services

This chapter demonstrates   **174**   Loading data

how to incorporate XML   **176**   Getting nodes

data into PHP scripts.   **178**   Getting attributes

180   Including feeds

182   Setting parameters

184   Selecting components

186   Summary

Loading data

There are many "Web Services" available online, which provide free data that can usefully be incorporated in your own web pages. Typical examples might supply live stock prices, the latest news stories, or current weather conditions.

Most Web Services offer to supply data in the XML (eXtensible Markup Language) file format. This is designed to be both human-readable and machine-readable and is not reliant upon any single platform. For example, a Java program can send XML data over the internet to a .NET application, and vice versa.

XML looks very much like HTML, but with XML you make up your own element names. The element tags surround content and may include attributes, as with HTML. It is important that each element has both opening and closing tags, and that elements are correctly nested for the XML document to be "well-formed".

All XML documents must begin with an XML file type declaration – like the one shown here on line 1.

catalog.xml

The **catalog.xml** file shown here will be used in the next few examples to demonstrate how to load XML data and how to access element values or attribute values.

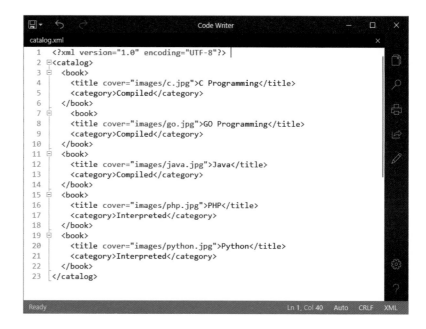

```xml
<?xml version="1.0" encoding="UTF-8"?>
<catalog>
  <book>
    <title cover="images/c.jpg">C Programming</title>
    <category>Compiled</category>
  </book>
  <book>
    <title cover="images/go.jpg">GO Programming</title>
    <category>Compiled</category>
  </book>
  <book>
    <title cover="images/java.jpg">Java</title>
    <category>Compiled</category>
  </book>
  <book>
    <title cover="images/php.jpg">PHP</title>
    <category>Interpreted</category>
  </book>
  <book>
    <title cover="images/python.jpg">Python</title>
    <category>Interpreted</category>
  </book>
</catalog>
```

PHP provides an XML parser called "SimpleXML" that can load an XML document into memory as a hierarchical tree structure. The **simplexml_load_file()** function requires the XML file name and path to transform the document into a data structure comprising "SimpleXMLElement" objects. The data structure can then be explored using the **var_dump()** function.

catalog.php

1 Begin a PHP script with a statement to set a page title and to preserve text formatting

```php
<?php
echo '<title>PHP SimpleXML</title><pre>' ;
```

2 Next, add a statement to load the XML data or quit

```php
$xml = simplexml_load_file( 'catalog.xml' )
or die( 'Unable to load data!' ) ;
```

3 Now, display all the SimpleXMLElement objects

```php
var_dump( $xml ) ;
```

4 Save the document in your web server's **/htdocs** directory as **catalog.php**, alongside the **catalog.xml** file, then open the page via HTTP to see the SimpleXMLElement objects

```
object(SimpleXMLElement)#1 (1) {
  ["book"]=>
  array(5) {
    [0]=>
    object(SimpleXMLElement)#2 (2) {
      ["title"]=>
      string(13) "C Programming"
      ["category"]=>
      string(8) "Compiled"
    }
    [1]=>
    object(SimpleXMLElement)#3 (2) {
      ["title"]=>
      string(14) "GO Programming"
      ["category"]=>
      string(8) "Compiled"
    }
    [2]=>
    object(SimpleXMLElement)#4 (2) {
      ["title"]=>
      string(4) "Java"
      ["category"]=>
      string(8) "Compiled"
    }
    [3]=>
    object(SimpleXMLElement)#5 (2) {
      ["title"]=>
      string(3) "PHP"
      ["category"]=>
      string(11) "Interpreted"
    }
    [4]=>
    object(SimpleXMLElement)#6 (2) {
      ["title"]=>
      string(6) "Python"
      ["category"]=>
      string(11) "Interpreted"
    }
  }
}
```

Notice that this data structure depicts an array named "book" that has five array elements – corresponding to the five XML **<book>** elements.

The ubiquitous nature of XML makes it ideal to transport data across the internet.

Getting nodes

The data structure contained in a SimpleXML object describes a parent-child relationship between outer and inner XML elements. Each member of the data structure is known as a "node". The top-level nodes are direct child descendants of the SimpleXML object itself, so can be referenced using the object name, **->** object operator, and child node name. For example, **$object->child**. A child of the child node (grandchild) can be referenced by adding a further **->** object operator, and the grandchild node name, such as **$object->child->grandchild** and so on for each further generation:

nodes.php

Hot tip

As there are five "book" nodes on the same hierarchical level, in this example they are created as an array. Each node can therefore be individually referenced using its node name and array index number.

1 Begin a PHP script with a statement to set a page title
```
<?php
echo '<title>PHP SimpleXML</title>' ;
```

2 Add a statement to load the XML data or quit
```
$xml = simplexml_load_file( 'catalog.xml' )
or die( 'Unable to load data!' ) ;
```

3 Next, retrieve the content of the "title" element that is a child of the first "book" element
```
echo 'First book : '.
        $xml->book[0]->title.' in easy steps<br>' ;
```

4 Now, retrieve the content of the "category" element that is a child of the first "book" element
```
echo 'Language category : '.$xml->book[0]->category ;
```

5 Save the document in your web server's **/htdocs** directory as **nodes.php**, alongside the **catalog.xml** file, then open the page via HTTP to see the node content

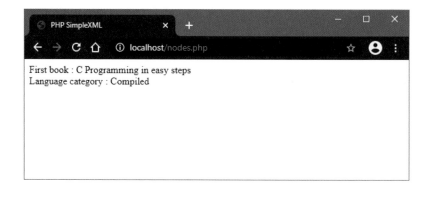

Looping through nodes

The SimpleXML object provides methods to work with the data contained within its data structure. Usefully, its **children()** method returns all child nodes and can be used to loop through the nodes to retrieve each node's content:

1 Begin a PHP script with a statement to set a page title
```
<?php
echo '<title>PHP SimpleXML</title>' ;
```

nodes-loop.php

2 Add a statement to load the XML data or quit
```
$xml = simplexml_load_file( 'catalog.xml' )
or die( 'Unable to load data!' ) ;
```

3 Next, initialize an iteration counter at zero
```
$counter = 0 ;
```

4 Now, add a loop to increment the counter and to display all "title" and "category" child node content
```
foreach( $xml->children() as $book )
{
  $counter++ ;
  echo 'Book '.$counter.' : ' ;
  echo $book->title.
  ' in easy steps ['.$book->category.']<hr>' ;
}
```

5 Save the document in your web server's **/htdocs** directory as **nodes-loop.php**, alongside the **catalog.xml** file, then open the page via HTTP to see all node content

177

Hot tip

Nested **foreach** loops can be used to traverse child nodes of each descendant generation.

PHP SimpleXML   ×   +   — □ ×

← → C ⟳ ⓘ localhost/nodes-loop.php   ☆ 😎 ⋮

Book 1 : C Programming in easy steps [Compiled]

Book 2 : GO Programming in easy steps [Compiled]

Book 3 : Java in easy steps [Compiled]

Book 4 : PHP in easy steps [Interpreted]

Book 5 : Python in easy steps [Interpreted]

Getting attributes

Values contained within attributes of a SimpleXMLElement object can be referenced by stating the attribute name, within quotes, between brackets following the node name. For example, **$object->child['feature']** accesses the value within an attribute named "feature" of a top-level "child" element:

attribs.php

 Begin a PHP script with a statement to set a page title
```
<?php
echo '<title>PHP SimpleXML</title>' ;
```

 Add a statement to load the XML data or quit
```
$xml = simplexml_load_file( 'catalog.xml' )
or die( 'Unable to load data!' ) ;
```

 Next, retrieve the content of the "title" element that is a child of the first "book" element
```
echo 'First book : '.
        $xml->book[0]->title.' in easy steps<br>' ;
```

 Now, display the value of the "cover" attribute of the "title" element that is a child of the first "book" element
```
echo 'Cover : '.$xml->book[0]->title['cover'].'<br>' ;
```

 Use the value retrieved in the previous step to display a cover image for the first "book" element
```
echo '<img src="'.$xml->book[0]->title['cover'].'">' ;
```

 Save the document in your web server's **/htdocs** directory as **nodes.php**, alongside the **catalog.xml** file, then open the page via HTTP to see the attribute value and image

Notice that each attribute value here is the path and filename to an image in a directory at **/htdocs/images**.

c.jpg

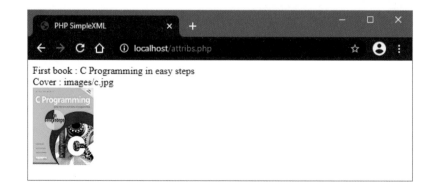

...cont'd

Looping through attributes

The SimpleXML object **children()** method can once again be used to loop through nodes and retrieve the value in a specified attribute of a particular node on each iteration:

1 Begin a PHP script with a statement to set a page title
```
<?php
echo '<title>PHP SimpleXML</title>' ;
```

attribs-loop.php

2 Add a statement to load the XML data or quit
```
$xml = simplexml_load_file( 'catalog.xml' )
or die( 'Unable to load data!' ) ;
```

3 Next, initialize an iteration counter at zero
```
$counter = 0 ;
```

4 Now, add a loop to increment the counter and to display its value, then retrieve an attribute value on each iteration to display an image
```
foreach( $xml->children() as $book )
{
  $counter++ ;
  echo ' '.$counter.': ' ;
  echo '<img src="'.$book->title['cover'].'">' ;
}
```

A SimpleXMLElement object also provides an **attributes()** method that returns an associative array of all attribute names and values within an element – for example, **$obj->child->attributes()**.

5 Save the document in your web server's **/htdocs** directory as **attribs-loop.php**, alongside the **catalog.xml** file, then open the page via HTTP to see the counter and image displayed on each iteration of the loop

c.jpg
go.jpg
java.jpg
php.jpg
python.jpg

You can discover more about RSS feeds online at **rssboard.org**

You can search for free RSS/XML news feeds to extract regularly updated news items with PHP.

The tags highlighted here can be used to retrieve the data of most interest. The item tags shown collapsed each also contain pubDate and inverseDescription, elements describing each item.

Including feeds

With the ability to access data from XML documents within PHP scripts, as described on the previous pages, we can easily incorporate data from external sources.

Many Web Services are offered as freely available RSS (Rich Site Summary/Really Simple Syndication) feeds. An online search for "rss feed directory" will provide a number of websites where links to free feeds are categorized. RSS feeds deliver regularly updated data in XML format.

Similarly, some Web Services are otherwise simply offered as "feeds" in XML or JSON (JavaScript Object Notation) format.

The FloatRates website offers lots of free feeds with currency exchange information at **www.floatrates.com/feeds.html** These provide exchange rates in XML (and JSON) format that are updated each day. For example, the US dollar (USD) feed is an XML document at **http://www.floatrates.com/daily/usd.xml**

XML feeds are typically documents containing a **<channel>** element, enclosing **<item>** elements that, in turn, enclose nested inner elements containing data:

```
1  <?xml version="1.0" encoding="utf-8"?>
2  <?xml-stylesheet type="text/xsl" href="http://www.floatrates.com/currency-rates.xsl" ?>
3  <channel>
4      <title>XML Daily Foreign Exchange Rates for U.S. Dollar (USD)</title>
5      <link>http://www.floatrates.com/currency/usd/</link>
6      <xmlLink>http://www.floatrates.com/daily/usd.xml</xmlLink>
7      <description>XML Daily foreign exchange rates for U.S. Dollar (USD)</description>
8      <language>en</language>
9      <baseCurrency>USD</baseCurrency>
10     <pubDate>Mon, 4 Jan 2023 00:00:01 GMT</pubDate>
11     <lastBuildDate>Mon, 4 Jan 2023 00:00:01 GMT</lastBuildDate>
12     <item>
13         <title>1 USD = 0.81565563 EUR</title>
14         <link>http://www.floatrates.com/usd/eur/</link>
15         <description>1 U.S. Dollar = 0.81565563 Euro</description>
16         <pubDate>Mon, 4 Jan 2023 00:00:01 GMT</pubDate>
17         <baseCurrency>USD</baseCurrency>
18         <baseName>U.S. Dollar</baseName>
19         <targetCurrency>EUR</targetCurrency>
20         <targetName>Euro</targetName>
21         <exchangeRate>0.81565563</exchangeRate>
22         <inverseRate>1.22600760</inverseRate>
23         <inverseDescription>1 Euro = 1.22600760 U.S. Dollar</inverseDescription>
24     </item>
25     <item...>
38     <item...>
51     <item...>
64     <item...>
77     <item...>
90     <item...>
103    <item...>
116    <item...>
129    <item...>
142    <item...>
155    <item...>
```

...cont'd

1 Begin a PHP script with a statement to load XML data from an external feed, or quit

```php
<?php
$url = 'http://www.floatrates.com/daily/usd.xml' ;
$xml =
simplexml_load_file( $url ) or die( 'Unable to load data!' ) ;
```

feed.php

2 Next, add a statement to load a page header file

```php
include( 'includes/feed-header.html' ) ;
```

feed-header.html

3 Now, add a statement to display the publication date

```php
echo '<p>'.$xml->pubDate.'</p>' ;
```

4 Then, display the first five exchange rates

```php
$i=1 ;
foreach ( $xml->item as $item )
{
  echo '<li>'.$item->inverseDescription ;
  $i++ ;
  if ($i > 5) break ;
}
```

5 Finally, add a statement to load a page footer file

```php
include( 'includes/feed-footer.html' ) ;
```

feed-footer.html

6 Save the document in your web server's **/htdocs** directory as **rss.php** then open the page via HTTP to see the rates

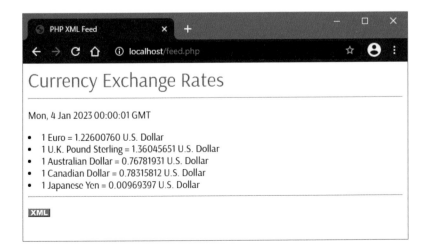

xml.png

PHP XML Feed

localhost/feed.php

Currency Exchange Rates

Mon, 4 Jan 2023 00:00:01 GMT

- 1 Euro = 1.22600760 U.S. Dollar
- 1 U.K. Pound Sterling = 1.36045651 U.S. Dollar
- 1 Australian Dollar = 0.76781931 U.S. Dollar
- 1 Canadian Dollar = 0.78315812 U.S. Dollar
- 1 Japanese Yen = 0.00969397 U.S. Dollar

XML

Discover more about OpenWeatherMap at **openweathermap.org** and sign up to receive your own ID key.

Setting parameters

Some Web Services provide a static URL, like the FloatRates feed in the previous example, that simply delivers XML data predetermined by the content supplier. Other Web Services provide a more flexible API (Application Programming Interface) that allows you to specify parameters in the URL request to determine what data you will receive, and in which format.

OpenWeatherMap has a free Current Weather Data API that can be found at **http://api.openweathermap.org/data/2.5/forecast** The Current Weather Data API allows you to request weather data in many forms. The parameters provided by this API include:

- **q** = city name (or city name, country code).

- **units** = metric (Celsius), imperial (Fahrenheit), or standard (Kelvin, the default) temperature scale.

- **mode** = xml, html, or json (the default) format.

- **appid** = required authorization key, supplied free upon registration at OpenWeatherMap.

The parameters and required = values are appended to the OpenWeatherMap URL after a **?** and are separated by **&**.

The response from OpenWeatherMap can be delivered as an XML file that may be written into the web server's **/htdocs** folder using the PHP **asXml()** function to specify a filename. This can be examined in the web browser to discover the nature of the data retrieved, the XML element names, attribute names and structure:

param.php

 Begin a PHP script by assigning string values to four variables, which will be used to set response parameters

```
<?php
$city = 'New York' ;
$units = 'imperial' ;
$mode = 'xml' ;
$id = '28df3c64f387cf55026e0de3fb8beaa4' ;
```

2 Next, add a statement to build a request string using specified parameter values

```
$request =
'http://api.openweathermap.org/data/2.5/forecast?'.
'q='.$city.'&units='.$units.'&mode='.$mode.'&APPID='.$id ;
```

3 Now, add a statement to load XML data using the request string parameters, or quit
$xml = simplexml_load_file($request)
or die('Unable to load data!') ;

4 When a response is received, attempt to write the content as an XML file in the web server's **/htdocs** directory
```
try
{
  $xml->asXml( 'params.xml' ) ;
  // Statement to be inserted here (Step 5).
}
catch( Exception $e )
{
  echo 'Error : '.$e->getMessage() ;
}
```

params.xml

5 Insert a statement to relocate the browser to view the newly created XML document
header('Location: params.xml') ;

6 Save the PHP script in your web server's **/htdocs** directory as **params.php** then open the page via HTTP to examine the XML content of the retrieved response

The response will only contain weather data for prevailing conditions.

The data highlighted here is that of most interest. It can be retrieved using each containing element name and attribute name.

Selecting components

Having examined the response data retrieved from OpenWeatherMap on page 183, selected components can be dynamically incorporated into a PHP sticky form XML App:

 Begin a PHP script by loading a page header file to provide a banner image

```php
<?php
include( 'includes/weather-header.html' ) ;
```

weather.php

 Next, add a conditional test to see if the page has been opened by form submission

```php
if( $_SERVER[ 'REQUEST_METHOD' ] == 'POST' )
{
    // Statements to be inserted here (Steps 3-6).
}
```

Hot tip

Notice that a default city value is assigned in case the form is submitted without user input.

184

3 Inside the conditional test block, assign parameter string values to four variables

```php
$city = ( empty( $_POST[ 'city' ] ) ) ? "New York"
        : $_POST[ 'city' ] ;
$units = 'imperial' ;
$mode = 'xml' ;
$id = '28df3c64f387cf55026e0de3fb8beaa4' ;
```

4 Next, inside the conditional test block, insert a statement to build a request string using specified parameter values

```php
$request =
'http://api.openweathermap.org/data/2.5/weather?'.
'q='.$city.'&units='.$units.'&mode='.$mode.'&APPID='.$id ;
```

5 Now, inside the conditional test block, insert a statement to load XML data using the parameters, or quit

```php
$xml = simplexml_load_file( $request )
or die( 'Unable to load data!' ) ;
```

Hot tip

The value of the **icon** attribute is the name of a PNG image file. When concatenated to the path and **.png** file extension, it provides an appropriate weather image.

6 Finally, insert statements to output retrieved data

```php
$icon = 'http://openweathermap.org/img/w/'.
        $xml->weather[ 'icon' ].'.png' ;
echo '<h1>Today in '.$xml->city[ 'name' ] ;
echo ' it\'s '.$xml->weather[ 'value' ].
        '<img src='.$icon.'></h1>' ;
echo '<ul><li>Temperature : '.$xml->temperature['value'] ;
echo '&deg; '.$xml->temperature[ 'unit' ] ;
echo '<li>Wind : '.$xml->wind->speed[ 'name' ] ;
echo '<li>Humidity : '.$xml->humidity['value'].'&#37;</ul>' ;
```

7 After the test block, add statements to create a form
```
echo '<form method="POST" action="weather.php">' ;
echo '<fieldset><legend>Enter City Name</legend>' ;
echo '<input type="text" name="city">' ;
echo '<input type="submit"
        name="submission" value = "Get Weather">' ;
echo '</fieldset></form>' ;
```

The **action** attribute specifies this script file to make the form sticky.

8 Finally, in the script, load a page footer file to display icons denoting the technologies employed by this app
```
include( 'includes/weather-footer.html' ) ;
```

9 Save the PHP script in your web server's **/htdocs** directory as **weather.php** then open the page via HTTP and submit the form to see weather for the default New York location. Enter another city name and resubmit to see that city's weather report

weather-header.html
weather-footer.html

iesweather.png
tech.png

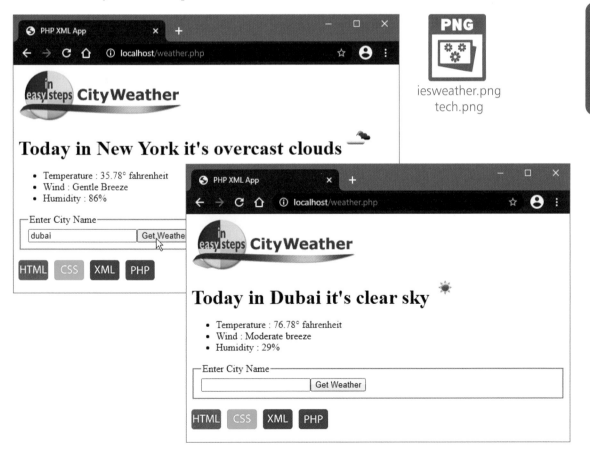

Summary

- XML elements must each have an opening and closing tag and be correctly nested to be well-formed.

- PHP has an XML parser called SimpleXML that can load an XML document into memory as a hierarchical tree structure.

- The **simplexml_load_file()** function creates a data structure of SimpleXMLElement objects.

- The data structure of a SimpleXML object describes a parent-child relationship between outer and inner XML elements.

- Each member of a SimpleXML data structure is a node.

- Top-level nodes are direct child descendants of the SimpleXML object itself.

- Nodes can be referenced using the **->** object operator to address each generation of the hierarchical tree structure.

- The **children()** method returns all child nodes and can be used to loop through tree nodes to retrieve each node's content.

- Attributes can be referenced by stating the attribute name, within quotes, between brackets following the node name.

- RSS feeds deliver regularly updated data in XML format.

- XML feeds are typically XML documents containing a top-level **<channel>** element that encloses **<item>** elements.

- Web Services may provide a static URL or an API that allows you to specify parameters in the URL request.

- Parameter values are specified by an **=** character and are appended to a URL after a **?** and are separated by an **&**.

- A SimpleXML object can be written as an XML file on the server using the **asXml()** function.

- Selected components of a SimpleXML object can be dynamically incorporated into a PHP application.

Index

Symbols

$ variable name operator	26
+ addition operator	44
( ) arguments operator	76
[ ] array element operator	30
=> array operator	30
= assignment operator	26
& bitwise AND operator	52
~ bitwise NOT operator	52
| bitwise OR operator	52
<< bitwise shift left operator	52
>> bitwise shift right operator	52
^ bitwise XOR operator	52
. concatenation operator	28
-- decrement operator	54
/ division operator	44
== equality operator	46
\ escape operator	28
** exponentiation operator	44
{ } function block operator	74
> greater operator	46
>= greater or equal operator	46
=== identicality operator	46
++ increment operator	54
!= inequality operator	46
<> inequality operator	46
< less operator	46
<= less or equal operator	46
&& logical AND operator	50
! logical NOT operator	50
|| logical OR operator	50
" mixed string operator	28
% modulus operator	44
* multiplication operator	44
!== non-identicality operator	46
?? null coalescing operator	48
?-> nullsafe operator	120
-> object operator	176
( ) precedence operator	44
{ } quoted key operator	34
<=> spaceship operator	46
' string operator	28
- subtraction operator	44
?: ternary operator	48

A

Abstract Syntax Tree	20
Abyss Web Server	9
configuration for PHP	14
installation	10
accessor methods, setter and getter	108
access specifiers	106
private	106
protected	106
public	106
action attribute (HTML)	138, 148
addition operator +	44
AND operator &&	50
appending text	130
arguments	76
arithmetic operators	44
+ addition	44
/ division	44
** exponentiation	44
% modulus	44
* multiplication	44
- subtraction	44
array	
elements	34
index	34
multi-dimensional	34
sorting	32
variable	30
array() function	30
arsort() function	32
ASCII code value	92
asort() function	32
Assembly language code	22
assignment operator =	26
asXml() function	182

B

backslash escape character \	28
base class	116
benchmark	23
binary number	52

bitwise operators
   & AND   52
   ~ NOT   52
   | OR   52
   << Shift left   52
   >> Shift right   52
   ^ XOR   52
Boolean values
   TRUE FALSE   50
break keyword   62, 70, 72
byte, 8 bits   52

C

callable   86
cascading style sheet (CSS)   155
case keyword   62
case-sensitivity   26, 74
catching exceptions
   try catch block   134
chain calls and properties   120
child node   176
class
   base   116
   declaration   106
   derived   116
   instance   107
   member   106
   method   106
      setter and getter   108
cloud (server-side)   9
comment rules   19
comparison operators
   == equality   46
   > greater than   46
   >= greater than or equal to   46
   === identicality   46
   != inequality   46
   <> inequality   46
   < less than   46
   <= less than or equal to   46
   !== non-identicality   46
   <=> spaceship   46
Compiling   20
concatenation   28
conditional branching   60
   case, break, default keywords   62, 72
   if, else keywords   58, 60, 72
   match keyword   64
   switch keyword   62, 64
conditional operator ?:   48
constant values   38

constructor method   112
   property promotion   114
continue keyword   71-72
cookie files   160
   getting data   162
   setting data   161
count() function   33
ctype_alnum() function   161
ctype_alpha() function   167
curly braces
   for function blocks   74
   for named array elements   34
Current Weather Data API   182

D

data hiding   106
data types   26
   union type   86
date and time
   date_default_timezone_get() function   100
   date_default_timezone_set() function   100
   date() function   100
declaring
   classes   106
   derived classes   116
decrement operator --   54
default keyword   62
define() function   38
derived class   116
destructor method   112
division operator /   44
double quotes
   variable substitution   26
do while loop   66, 68

E

echo instruction   17
element   30
elseif keyword   60
else keyword   60, 72
empty() function   142
encapsulation   107
encoding
   HTML entities   102
equality operator ==   46
error handling
   custom error_handler() function   132

try catch block	134
escape \ backslash character	28
Exception class	
getFile() method	134
getLine() method	134
getMessage() method	134
eXclusive OR operator xor	50
explode() function	32
exponentiation operator **	44

F

FALSE Boolean value	48, 50, 56
fclose() function	124
feof() function	126
fgetc() function	127
fgets() function	126
file extension .php	14
file modes	124
filesize() function	124
filestream object	124
footer file inclusion	154
fopen() function	124
foreach loop	30, 66
for loop	66
form data	138
fread() function	124
functions	
creating	74
passing arguments	76

G

GET request method	139, 148
getter methods, class	108
global scope	82
greater than operators	
> greater than	46
>= greater than or equal to	46
group expressions	44

H

header file inclusion	154
header() function	161, 167
Hello World! script	16

htdocs directory	11
HTML entities	
htmlentities(), htmlspecialchars()	102
HTML form	138
action attribute	138
hidden fields	146
method attribute	138
sticky fields	150
HTML <form> tag	138
HTML hyperlink	
appending data	156
HTTP Hypertext Transfer Protocol	9

I

identicality operator ===	46
if else statement	60
if keyword	58
implode() function	32
include() function	154
includes folder	155
increment operator ++	54
inequality operator !=	46
inequality operator <>	46
inheritance	116
instance, class	107
multiple objects	110
is_array() function	32
isset() function	140, 150, 160, 162, 166
iteration loop	66

J

Just In Time (JIT) compilation	22

K

key name	30
krsort() function	32
ksort() function	32

189

L

Least Significant Bit (LSB)	52
length strlen()	92
less than operators	
< less than	46
<= less than or equal to	46
Lexing	20
localhost domain (127.0.0.1)	11, 14
local scope	82
logical operators	
and Logical AND	50
&& Logical AND	50
! Logical NOT	50
|| Logical OR	50
or Logical OR	50
xor Logical eXclusive OR	50
loops	
break keyword	70
continue keyword	71
do keyword	68
foreach keyword	66
for keyword	66
while keyword	68
ltrim() function	98

M

match keyword	64
md5() function	161
members, class	106
method attribute (HTML)	138
methods, class	106
setter and getter	108
mixed string	
variable substitution with double quotes	26, 28
modulus operator %	44
Most Significant Bit (MSB)	52
multi-dimensional arrays	34
multiplication operator *	44

N

named parameters	80
naming conventions	26, 76
accessor methods	108
class destructor	112
classes	106
nested loop	66
non-identicality operator !==	46
NOT operator !	50
null coalescing operator ??	48
nullsafe operator ?->	120
NULL value	140

O

object	107
object operator ->	176
Object Oriented Programming (OOP)	106
encapsulation	106
inheritance	116
polymorphism	118
OPcache	20
OPcode	20
OpenWeatherMap	182
operators	
arithmetical + - * / % **	44
bitwise & | ~ ^ << >>	52
comparison == != <> === !== > < >= <= ?:	46
logical && and || or xor !	50
ord() function	92
OR operator ||	50

P

parameters	76
named	80, 90
positional	80
Parsing	20
PHP	
case-sensitivity	26
embedding code	16
file extension .php	15
functions	74
installation	12
introduction	8

tags <?php ?>	16
variables	26
phpinfo() function	15
polymorphism	118
positional parameters	80
POST request method	138, 148
preg_match() function	142, 167
private, access specifier	106
property promotion	114
protected, access specifier	106
public, access specifier	106

Q

quotation marks	26

R

regular expression	142
REQUEST_METHOD element	148
require() function	154
rsort() function	32
RSS (Really Simple Syndication) feeds	180
rtrim() function	98
rules	
tags, statements, comments	18-19

S

server console	11
sessions	
getting data	168
session_destroy() function	170
session_id() function	170
session_start() function	166
setting data	167
unset() function	170
setcookie() function	160-161
set_error_handler() function	132
setter methods, class	108
SimpleXMLElement object	
children() method	177, 179
node attributes	178
nodes	176
simplexml_load_file() function	174
SimpleXML parser	174

single document form submission	148
single quotes	28
sort() function	32
spaceship operator <=>	46
statement rules	19
sticky forms	150
strcasecmp() function	92
strchr() function	94
strcmp() function	92
str_contains() function	94
str_ends_with() function	94
string	
changing case	97
comparison	92
formatting	98
searching	94
trimming	98
strings	28
stristr() function	94
strlen() function	92
strncasecmp() function	92
strncmp() function	92
strpad() function	98
strpos() function	94
strrchr() function	94
strrev() function	98
strrpos() function	94
strrpt() function	98
str_starts_with() function	94
strstr() function	94
strtok() function	98
strtotime() function	100
style sheet	155
substr_count() function	96
substr() function	96
substr_replace() function	96
subtraction operator -	44
superglobals	
$_COOKIE	162, 164
$_GET array	156
$_POST	166
$_POST array	138, 150, 156
$_SERVER array	148
$_SESSION	166-167
$_SESSION array	156
switch keyword	62

T

tag rules	18
ternary operator ?:	48
text	28
throw keyword	134
title	154
tokens	20
trigger_error() function	132
trim() function	98
TRUE Boolean value	48, 50, 56
try catch block	134

U

unary operator	50
union type	86
uppercase constant names	38

V

value attribute	150
var_dump() function	164, 170, 174
variable	26
scope	82

W

Web Services	174
API (Application Programming Interface)	182
RSS feed directory	180
while loop	66, 68
writing files	
fwrite()	128

X

XML App	184
XML (eXtensible Markup Language)	174

Z

Zend Virtual Machine	20
zero-based index	34